2.00

P9-CMA-721

In the Footsteps of the Mystics

A GUIDE TO THE SPIRITUAL CLASSICS

Henry C. Simmons

Paulist Press/New York/Mahwah, N.J.

Library of Congress Cataloging-in-Publication Data

Simmons, Henry C.
    In the footsteps of the mystics: a guide to the spiritual classics/
Henry C. Simmons.
        p. cm.
    Includes bibliographical references.
    ISBN 0-8091-0457-1
    1. Spirituality.   2. Spirituality—Study and teaching.
    3. Classics of Western spirituality.   I. Title.
    BV4501.2.S4712   1991
    248—dc20   91-39215
                                                                          CIP

Published by Paulist Press
997 Macarthur Boulevard
Mahwah, NJ 07430

Printed and bound in the
United States of America

Contents

For Helen M. Simmons, my mother, whose pursuit of knowledge encourages my search for a wider vision.

Preface

*T*his book began in 1989 with a visit by Peter Ainslie, a Disciples of Christ minister serving a church in Bethesda, Maryland. Peter spoke of his dream to engage adults, particularly older adults, in reading and reflecting on the mystics— those people whose writings we find in the Classics of Western Spirituality. In the course of our conversation we found that our interests coalesced wonderfully: I was already working with a set of questions which helped organize the material, and Peter had actually begun selecting quotations from the mystics.

Over the next year, Peter and I each met with groups of adults, listening to their interests, trying various selections from the Classics, discovering that arranging them according to personality type helped people get into the texts. In this part of the project, it was Peter's enthusiasm, determination, and outgoing pastoral manner that kept the project moving forward. Without him, this book, which is the result of our joint effort, would never have come to be.

When the time came to actually write the book, Peter asked me to take full responsibility. I wrote and rewrote, made the final choice of texts, found new texts to round out our selections. Peter continued to do research, to discuss selections, and to use the material in his pastoral ministry. The book as we have it now is in form substantially different from what we had envisioned. Editors have a way of making that happen! But our enthusiasm to make the mystics more accessible to people who might describe themselves as "ordinary" remains at the heart of this book.

I am deeply grateful to Peter Ainslie, colleague and co-worker, for all he has given.

Henry C. Simmons
Richmond, Virginia

Introduction

T he purpose of this book is to introduce the reader to a wide variety of authors whose writings are known collectively as the Classics of Western Spirituality. It is "by way of introduction" and is a gentle invitation to you to meet some of God's friends and to let them become your companions on your journey. Without their insights our lives are less rich, our ways of speaking about God less adequate, our challenge to growth less acute, our delight in the things of God less sure. Devotional writings of the present day are not enough to nourish the spirit adequately. Even the words of the scriptures can come to new life when seen through the eyes of others of God's friends.

At one level, it may seem unnecessary to "introduce" the Classics of Western Spirituality. These books are widely available in good contemporary translations with ample notes in the collection published by Paulist Press; and indeed in their paperback format they are very inexpensive. But the simple fact is that these texts are virtually unknown to the vast majority of adult believers. Beautiful, powerful, important reflections on the spiritual life, written by some of God's close friends and lovers, are somehow lost to ordinary folk who themselves struggle with the same questions and rejoice in the same love of God as did these authors.

If these authors are so important, why are they not widely read? It is daunting, even disheartening, to face a series of more than seventy books—the Classics of Western

Spirituality. Where does one begin? What do we really have in common with these authors from centuries so different from ours? We recognize the difficulties. But we are so in love with and enthusiastic about the insights of a variety of authors that we persist in trying to make our introductions.

We trust that the organization of this book facilitates the process. First, we have organized our selections of relatively short quotations from a wide variety of texts around a series of questions which you will recognize as your own—questions that reflective people answer for themselves as they try to be faithful in their lives with God. These are questions such as: "What is the relationship between the love of God and the love of neighbor?" "What is sin?" "How do I best pray?" "Where is the presence of God to be found?"[1] For each question we invite your response, and then share with you some answers to that same question by a dozen or more authors whose writings are part of the Classics of Western Spirituality. We invite your thoughtful reading of their answers, and encourage a conversation between your answer and theirs.

There are limitations to this approach. The authors we are quoting lived over a span of seventeen or eighteen centuries, and their understandings were profoundly shaped by the cultures in which they lived, the languages they spoke, their religious and denominational affiliations. We are not frightened off by the limitations of our approach, however. Simply, the texts are so wonderfully compelling, so beautiful, so uplifting, so challenging that we are content to work

---

1. We have developed various lists of questions. Two such lists are found in Appendix A. No list pretends to cover the whole of the spiritual life, and the reader is encouraged to add to them, and to respond to the questions in any order which seems helpful.

with limitations. For example, when we read the following words they resonate with our experience; somehow they encourage us in the quest for God. "The first [consideration for anyone who wishes to be intimate with God] is that friendship and communion with God are possible in this life of exile. This friendship is not remote but more sure and intimate than ever existed between brothers or even between mother and child. [. . .] This communion is more certain than anything else in the world, and nothing is more joyous, more valuable, or more precious." Or when we read these words, we are moved deeply by an insight into God's graciousness: "Love where you may, you will have loved Him;[2] turn your face whatever way, it turns toward Him—even if you know it not. [. . .] The beauty of each lovely boy, each comely girl derives from Him—on loan." It does not matter to us that one text was written by a sixteenth-century Christian (a member of the Franciscan Order), the other by a thirteenth-century Muslim (a Sufi mystic)—these are God's friends and lovers; these are worthy companions for our journey. Nor does it matter that their names are strange to us and perhaps difficult to pronounce: Francisco de Osuna and Fakhruddin ʿIraqi.[3] Their questions and ours are similar enough that we can reach across the ages, can take them as our companions, and even perhaps become lifelong friends. This, then, is the first way in which we have organized this book in order to make readily available some of the words of God's friends:

---

2. We wrestled with whether or not to change God language and references to people to make them gender inclusive. We decided to leave the texts the way they are written and translated to allow texts which do deal inclusively with God and people to stand out. We strongly recommend that in reading the texts privately or aloud you be free to change language as you will.

3. A complete list of authors cited appears in Appendix B. For each there is a very brief historical note.

We have selected short quotations from a variety of authors in answer to questions which are the common coin of the devout life.

The second principle of organization is somewhat more complex and will be developed in the first chapter. At this point, we will simply give a brief indication. The insight with which we began will make clear in some initial way what we have attempted. We have observed that there are some approaches to the spiritual life which seem so foreign to us, even so abrasive to our way of approaching God that we simply lose heart when we begin to try the proposed path. Sometimes this is discouraging—our friends tell us we ought to read this or that book, do this or that spiritual exercise, but we simply cannot get engaged. We may even begin to wonder what is wrong with us! People are very different in their approaches to prayer, in their paths to God. We have organized this book to respect such differences.

Following the insights of Urban T. Holmes as he tries to describe what patterns of spirituality "look like," we have identified two areas in which important differences occur. First, some people approach God more with the mind than with the heart others approach God more with the heart than with the mind. One or other of these approaches is likely to be dominant at any time. Second, some find that they pray best by using images; others find that they pray best when they empty themselves of images. Some people use techniques of engaging the senses in image-rich meditation; others prefer techniques of emptying the senses in contemplation which abandons images. Together, these two important differences yield four approaches to God in prayer: heart/imaging, mind/imaging, heart/emptying of images, mind/emptying of images.

We may get a small sense of how profoundly these differences affect a person's approach by comparing the following quotations. Jacob Boehme writes: "The student said: 'How can I hear when I remain silent in thinking and willing?' The master said: 'When you remain silent from the thinking and willing of self, the eternal hearing, seeing and speaking will be revealed in you, and God will see and hear through you. Your own hearing, willing and seeing hinders you so that you do not see and hear God.' " In a quite different approach, John Cassian writes: "Oh, how delightful to the soul and pleasing to me is holy prayer made in the house of self-knowledge and knowledge of me!." One author sees self-knowledge and self-understanding as hindering the approach to God; the other sees self-knowledge as the house in which holy prayer is made.

It is probably not beneficial to go into more detail here. For many people with whom we have shared our insights and our organization of the writings, this fourfold division has been useful. It has, in the first place, steered people toward writings with which they were more likely to be "at home" and it has clarified why others seem so distant, uninviting, and challenging. We think this organization is helpful, but we are aware of limitations. Some writings admit of this classification more easily than do others; at times we have been quite sure where a text belonged, at times quite unsure. No doubt you will differ with our classification more than once in the course of this book. We also recognize that by attempting such classification of texts we have inevitably omitted texts which might have been wonderfully enriching. In the final analysis we leave it to you to decide the helpfulness of this organization of texts. We have used it in an attempt to make more accessible the words of some of God's friends who we hope will be your companions on the journey. To the extent that it does so, it is worthwhile.

This book is intended for anyone who is (or is becoming)

thoughtful about the spiritual life. The questions addressed in the text are, as we have indicated, common-coin questions of the devout life; the invitation to consider these questions in a more thoroughgoing way will appeal to a wide variety of people. In particular, we hope that some who have found that the resources currently available are not nourishing their spirits or sufficiently helping them live out their beliefs will delight in the rich resources of the Classics of Western Spirituality. Those for whom the text is intended include people who have worked for a long time at meditation and prayer, who have tried to live disciplined lives, who have profited from conversation with peers about the quest for God. Their maturity in the spiritual life is real—a maturity born of constancy and fidelity to questions and issues which characterize the spiritual life. This book is an invitation to look again at these questions and to compare their life-answers with those of the writers represented in the Classics of Western Spirituality. Equally, this text is an invitation to those for whom questions of the spiritual life are becoming real for the first time. These are people who are becoming concerned about the spiritual life for whatever reason, and who need in a particular way the companionship of others who have sought answers to important questions.

There is one age group to which we address this book in a particular way, namely, those who are the elders in our midst—people in their sixties, seventies, eighties, nineties. We can only speculate why the sorts of questions we are addressing here are so persistent for many of them. Were the generations now over sixty-five more religious in their growing up years? Probably so. Many of these people grew up with questions that are now coming to fruition. It may also be that long years of retirement, now being experienced by large numbers for the first time in history, are giving new scope to what Erik Erikson has identified as the final "age" of human life. The challenge now is to put one's life together so that there is a sense of integration rather than a sense of despair—to see that one's life has real meaning. The companionship of God's friends can be for them a powerful sustaining reality.

In our preparation of this text we worked closely with many groups, comprised of individuals young and old. It was a particular delight to see flourish a sense of excitement and, indeed, competence among those for whom there has been precious little in the way of substantial resources for the devout life. It was also wonderfully encouraging to find in these materials the basis for group discussion and conversation about topics of common interest and passion among adults of a wide range of ages.

We do not intend this book to be used passively. It is not a matter simply of reading what other people have said about important things. When we use the image of "companion" we anticipate that it is possible for us to share with people across the years, even though they are not at our side to respond. We are familiar with the idea of "talking to God" in prayer. Sometimes we "hear God speak to us" in our meditations. At other times we can only claim that our lives are shaped by our prayer, that we leave the place of prayer more sure, more quiet, more energized, more humble, more loving. We have been moved by companionship with God and God's friends. We recognize that this is not "companionship" or "conversation" in the ordinary sense of a long chat with a friend. But surely this is, at some level a two-way dialogue. Our awareness of the presence of the Other lets us touch the hidden or deep parts of ourselves from which we draw the strength to change or grow.

We may, in a similar fashion, experience the presence of a parent, grandparent or spouse who is now dead. They are so present that we may find ourselves talking with them, and we may find this companionship comforting or healing in spite of its obvious limitations.

From our experience and that of others, we know it is possible to enter into conversation and to find companionship with those who have gone before us in the faith. It is for this reason that we invite you to meet some of God's friends and let them become your companions on your journey.

In Appendix C we make suggestions for using these texts individually and in groups. In particular we hope to help individuals and groups get started, and to that end we suggest two preliminary exercises to assist people to get in touch with their personal spiritual journeys. Even reflective individuals may profit from some exercises to help them begin again to pay attention to their journeys, and to rediscover personal questions which have given rise to life-answers. Then we make suggestions for the actual use of the text by individuals and groups, which we have used this text fairly extensively. Some of our insights may prove helpful as you use this book.

We turn now to the first chapter. It introduces in a more thoroughgoing way the four approaches to the spiritual life and we invite you to spend some time becoming familiar with our fourfold division. It is our hope that you may use this book more easily and may feel more confident in deciding for yourself to what extent the use of this fourfold division is helpful in some measure in your discovery of the richness of the words of God's friends and your companions.

We remind our readers that Appendix C gives some suggestions for using this text. We also remind you that you may simply wish to delve right into the subject matter of chapters 2 and following. Again, we encourage you to use this book in the way that is best for you.

1. The Variety of Gifts

*W*hy does one person respond to a question about the spiritual life in one way, and another person answer the same question in quite a different manner? Personal experience is a powerful factor, as are church tradition, historical era, education, age, gender and social class. These factors may account for an array of answers too various to catalogue. Some, however, seem to fall into patterns which give us categories for understanding "the shape and flow of our relationship with God and [allow us to] identify our own place within the much wider [spiritual] tradition."[1]

What do patterns of spirituality look like? What do they describe? As we look at two questions which are common to those who seek union with God—the goal of every spiritual quest—namely "Is your approach to God more a matter of the mind or of the heart?" and "How do you best pray?" we note that answers to each of these questions reveal a polarity. The question, "Is your approach to God more a matter of the mind or of the heart?" raises the question of whether the spiritual method emphasizes the illumination of the mind (speculative) or the heart or emotions (affective).[2] For exam-

---

1. Urban T. Holmes, III, *A History of Christian Spirituality*, New York: Seabury, 1980, p. 4. This insight, with the explanation that follows, is based on Holmes (ibid., pp. 3–5).
2. Holmes, p. 4.

ple, William Law clearly opts for the illumination of the mind (speculative) when he writes: "The greater any man's mind is, the more he knows of God and himself, the more will he be disposed to prostrate himself before God in all the humblest acts and expressions of repentance. [. . .] Now if devotion at these seasons is the effect of a better knowledge of God and ourselves, then the neglect of devotion at other times is always owing to great ignorance of God and ourselves" (pp. 343–44).

Answers to the question "How do you best pray?" reveal another polarity: Some ascetical or spiritual methods advocate the development of images in meditation, others advocate emptying techniques. Thus, for example, Jacob Boehme writes about the experience of prayer in image-rich language which fosters an imaginal technique: "To all hungering, repenting souls: [they] will discover properly within [themselves] how the old father of the prodigal son comes toward the poor, changed repentant soul and falls around the neck of its essence of life with His love, and with His love embraces and kisses it, grasping it in His arms, and speaking to it with power" (p. 75). In contrast, Gregory Palamas clearly suggests why an emptying technique is important in meditation when he speaks of an "unknowing": "Beyond the stripping away of beings, or rather after the cessation [of our perceiving or thinking of them] accomplished not only in words, but in reality, there remains an unknowing which is beyond knowledge" (p. 36).

Some seek illumination of the mind; others seek illumination of the heart. This is the first polarity: mind/heart. Some use techniques of engaging the senses in image-rich meditation, others use techniques of emptying the senses in contemplation which abandons images. This is the second polarity: imaging/emptying of images.[3] These polarities do not represent better or worse, right or wrong. They simply describe patterns and preferences which are likely to appear in spiritual or ascetical methods which assist the quest for union with God. On either scale an individual might find himself or herself strongly or weakly positioned toward one or other pole. An individual might also find himself or herself drawn toward one or other style depending on the particular time in his or her life, or on the circumstances in which the quest for union with God is being worked out. But as the old saying goes, "Everybody has to be somewhere," and these patterns, with the options they imply, do allow us to describe what an individual's spirituality "looks like."

This is all the more the case because both polarities function at the same time; thus two polarities yield four basic approaches to the spiritual life: heart/imaging, heart/emptying of images, mind/imaging, mind/emptying of images. One or other of these will best describe a starting point for the individual's quest for union with God. A graphic presentation of the four positions may help us to visualize options which define and characterize certain forms of spirituality.[4]

In this figure, two scales are portrayed and four approaches. But the circle itself also represents an attempt to hold together in tension all four approaches. Holmes calls

---

3. Some readers familiar with the Myers-Briggs typology may wish to explore the relationship between that typology and the two polarities presented. We refer them to Appendix D.

4. The mind/heart polarity may also be designated with its more technical terms, speculative/affective; the imaging/emptying of image polarity may also be designated with its technical terms, kataphatic/apophatic.

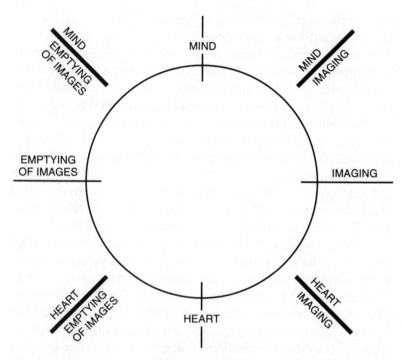

the circle a *circle of sensibility*.[5] This is a gracious phrase.
Most forms of spirituality will emphasize one of the four
approaches which result from the intersection of the polarities of heart/mind, images/emptying of images. But every
spirituality which is sensitive—that is, every spirituality
within this circle of sensibility—will respect all other spiri-
tualities, not only for what they are in themselves, but also
for what they offer to each other.

A sensitive spirituality will, however, maintain a
certain tension with those other dimensions that

---

5. Holmes, pp. 4–5.

are not emphasized as a corrective to an exaggerated form of prayer. "Sensibility" defines for us that sensitivity to the ambiguity of styles of prayer and the possibilities for a creative dialogue within the person and within the community as it seeks to understand the experience of God and its meaning for the world. Without that tension we fall into excesses.[6]

To the extent that we are strongly attracted to one of these approaches to the spiritual life (heart/images, heart/emptying of images, mind/images, mind/emptying of images) we will be less comfortable with the approach which is directly opposed to ours. We could adduce technical reasons for this but the simplest argument supporting this position is common experience. If, for example, we are strongly attracted to a heart/emptying of images approach, the Ignatian Exercises (or any imaginal technique of meditation which seeks illumination of the mind and will) will seem very foreign, dry, distracting, even offensive. This does not mean that such an approach should be avoided forever! We can readily guess that it will serve as a corrective to the heart/emptying of images approach. As Holmes rightly notes: "A sensitive spirituality will [. . .] maintain a certain tension with those other dimensions that are not emphasized as a corrective to an exaggerated form of prayer. [. . .] Without that tension we fall into excesses."[7]

While each approach to the spiritual life has validity, no single one is likely to prove adequate. The more we find ourselves drawn consistently toward one approach, the

---

6. Holmes, p. 5.
7. Holmes, p. 5.

more we need to have that approach challenged by its opposite. The person, for example, who is deeply rooted in an approach which stresses heart/images needs to learn of the absolute mystery which dwells in inaccessible light—a perspective emphasized by those whose approach is mind/emptying of images. Similarly, the one whose approach is heart/emptying of images needs to explore forms of meditation which seek illumination of the mind using imaginal techniques. By the use of the four approaches to the spiritual life based on these two polarities it is "possible to make comparisons [. . .] and to define spiritual practice and its immediate objectives with some clarity—the assumption being that in all methods the ultimate goal is union with God."[8] The identification of approaches also allows us to engage in conversation with less intimidation than if we simply took all the Classics of Western Spirituality as equally suited for us.

Preferred forms of approach to union with God may shift over the years as we mature and as the circumstances of our lives change. For example, people whose worlds have been shattered by unexplainable and unavoidable evil may—however imaginal their techniques of meditation had been—come to mistrust all the images of God which had given nourishment previously. Other people may, in the awakening of their ability to think and study come to rejoice in a hitherto untapped enthusiasm for the illumination of the mind through imaginal techniques. Nevertheless, many people find that there is one approach that, more than the other three, requires no "processing." Without any thought or effort, that approach seems compatible with one's natural

---

8. Ibid.

gifts. This does not keep us from needing, exploring, even rejoicing in, other approaches.

There are two additional points which may temper what has been proposed. First, the attentive reader will note that sometimes (although not often) one author will show up in more than one approach. How can this be? The quotations which we use are excerpts from longer pieces and there is a certain inevitable amount of distortion in lifting them out of context, and may account for variations. Also, authors who are mature may have fully developed and rich personalities which are comfortable with many approaches. Indeed, some authors seem intent on exploring unfamiliar territory, which accounts for some variations. In particular, as has been noted, authors whose initial approach to meditation is imaginal seem at some point to mistrust their images for God; their preference is tempered by a growing conviction of the unknowableness of God and the inadequacy of any image. Second, the selection and placing of quotations is subject to our interpretations. We have identified each quotation as fitting into a certain approach and our basis for selection was the text itself rather than the author. Overall, however, authors' words represent a particular approach to the spiritual life, and the proposed identification of four approaches is a powerful tool for engaging in conversation and companionship with others both like and unlike us.

We have said enough. We invite you now to come with us on a journey with some of God's friends. The journey is for you. It begins with attention to your own starting points so that in these conversations your voice will not be lost. Throughout this text we will invite you to reflect on your preferred approach, the lessons you have learned, the point of view you have reached as you mature. We invite you to take time to answer each question as it occurs. If it is well for you to do so, we invite you to commit that answer to writing so that you will know your starting point with some clarity and can watch as your perspectives emerge, develop and change.

With your reflections clear and your writing task accomplished, we invite you to listen to the reflections of sisters and brothers from other ages. Take the words of the companion into your mind and heart; test out within yourself how familiar and compatible they are to your experience; savor them graciously if they fit your experience; treat them respectfully if they do not. Let them put you in touch with new names for the experience of the presence of God. Do not be afraid to speak back to them, to hold your own truth. But do so with the respect that all the friends of God deserve.

2. Approaches to God

$\mathcal{W}$e turn now to the question: "Is your approach to God more a matter of the mind or of the heart?" First we invite you to spend a little time with your own thoughts. How have you answered this question in your life? Think of specific examples, remember times and events. The question is not abstract. As you will see in the texts, and quite probably in your own response, there is in this question a sense of *value decisions* about God. Some value decisions arise from a feeling approach, others from a thinking approach. Indeed, the question could even be asked: "Do you make decisions about God more with your mind or with your heart?" When you have gathered information from whatever inner or outer source, do you make value decisions about God based on reason or on feeling? For example, do you get in touch with God's will for you (and so follow that will) by a process of thoughtful discernment, or do you just "follow your heart" without ever being able to explain your reasons?

Jot down your reflections. They are an important part of you and are worthy of careful attention. Please don't let yourself engage in negative self-talk: "Oh, this is only me; what do I know; let's get on to people who are important. . . ." Listen with care to your own experience. It has been an important part of your life with God, and God's with you. When you have finished jotting down your reflections, please turn to the texts. We invite you to read them slowly and thoughtfully, beginning with those which represent the approach you feel is most like yours. It may be helpful to read the texts aloud. Enjoy the insights of these friends of God as they articulate their approach to God. Do more than this, though. As you become familiar with these texts, let their authors become your companions. If a word or phrase strikes you, note it, wonder how it enriches or challenges your approach. If it seems good to you, commit it to memory. If you feel comfortable, enter into conversation with these friends of God.

The first two sets of texts have been selected to emphasize the quest for the illumination of the heart as an important element in the approach to God. The sets differ in their preference for images or emptying of images. Thus, the first set is heart/imaging, the second is heart/emptying of images. The third and fourth sets of texts have been selected to emphasize illumination of the mind in the approach to God. These two sets also differ in their preference for images or emptying of images. Thus the third set is mind/imaging, and the fourth is mind/emptying of images. In all four sets of texts what is at stake is not simply an abstract preference for thinking or feeling but our personal ways of making value decisions about God.

As we have already discussed, each of us tends to favor one approach, although the degree of preference will vary. For some, the answer to this question will be crystal clear. For others, there may be a hesitancy to answer the question one way or another. For yet others there may be a sense that there has been a shift over the years from thinking to feeling or from feeling to thinking. If, as you work through these texts, you find yourself consistently preferring the texts of one set rather than another, you will probably be one whose approach is quite definite. If you find yourself consistently "repelled" (the word is hardly too strong for some) by the texts of one set, you are probably quite clearly in the opposite quadrant of the circle. If texts in all sets have an appeal for you, enjoy them all. Your variety of approaches opens you to a great diversity of companions for your journey to God.

Heart/imaging

Jacopone da Todi:
Love, Love, You have wounded me,
Your name only can I invoke;
Love, Love, I am one with You,
Let me embrace You alone.
Love, Love, You have swept me up violently,
My heart is beside itself with love;
I want to faint, Love; may I always be close to You:
Love, I beseech You, let me die of love.
. . .
Love, You are life—my soul cannot live without You;
Why do You make it faint, clasping it so tightly, Love?
(pp. 264–65).

Jacob Boehme: "If we did not know half as much, and were more childlike, but had only one brotherly will among one another, and lived as children of one mother, as twigs on one tree that all take sap from one root, we would be much holier" (p. 166).

"[To] all hungering, repenting souls. He will discover properly within himself how the old father of the prodigal son comes toward the poor, changed repentant soul and falls around the neck of its essence of life with His love, and with His love embraces and kisses it, grasping it in His arms, and speaking to it with power: 'This is my dear son: This is my

dear soul that I lost. It was dead and has come alive again' "
(p. 75).

Richard Rolle:
Love is the sweetest thing that man on earth has known;
Love is God's own darling; love binds by blood and
    bone.
In love be our liking, I know not a better home;
For me and my loving, by love we're both made one
    (p. 190).

Julian of Norwich: "For as truly as there is in God a
quality of pity and compassion, so truly is there in God a
quality of thirst and longing; and the power of this longing in
Christ enables us to respond to his longing, and without this
no soul comes to heaven. And this quality of longing and
thirst comes from God's everlasting goodness. And though
he may have both longing and pity, they are different qualities, as I see them; and this is the characteristic of spiritual
thirst, which will persist in him so long as we are in need,
and will draw us up into his bliss" (p. 231).

John Wesley:
Thou lov'st whate'er thy hands have made;
    Thy goodness we rehearse,
In shining characters displayed
    Throughout our universe.

Mercy, with love, and endless grace
    O'er all thy works doth reign;
But mostly thou delight'st to bless
    Thy favorite creature, man.

Wherefore let every creature give
To thee the praise designed;
But chiefly, Lord, the thanks receive,
The hearts of all mankind (pp. 206–7).

"In the evening, I went very unwillingly to a society in Aldersgate Street, where one was reading Luther's Preface to the Epistle to the Romans. About a quarter before nine, while he was describing the change which God works in the heart through faith in Christ, I felt my heart strangely warmed. I felt I did trust in Christ, Christ alone for salvation; and an assurance was given me that he had taken away my sins, even mine, and saved me from the law of sin and death" (p. 107).

Jacob Boehme: "O highest Love, You have appeared in me. Remain in me. Embrace me in Yourself. Keep me in You so that I cannot bend from You. Fill my hunger with Your love. Feed my soul with heavenly being and give it as drink the blood of my Redeemer Jesus Christ. Let it drink from Your fountain" (p. 49).

Francisco de Osuna: "This love consists of directing the will that is lovingly fixed on that highest good so that with the will affectionately gazing on God, the heart and being of man may rush to God more quickly than a stone falling to the center of the earth. Those practiced in love do this without their even considering it, for their natural love is alive and directed to God and they love him without forethought. As we are instinctively attracted to lovely, gracious things, so habitual affection is attracted to God and loves him sweetly, sometimes even before it thinks about him. Love, which by now operates by itself, usually awakens the proficient to love because things that by nature attract love awaken love for

God; this happens with songs, joys, beauty, lovely fra-
grances, flowers, and music" (pp. 441–42).

Fakhruddin ʿIraqi:
In those days
     before a trace
of the two worlds,
     no "other" yet imprinted
on the Tablet of Existence,
     I, the Beloved, and Love
lived together
     in the corner
of an uninhabited
     cell.

But suddenly Love the Unsettled flung back the curtain
from the whole show, to display Its perfection as the "Beloved" before the entity of the world;

and when Its ray of loveliness appeared
at once the world came into being
at once the world borrowed sight
from Love's Beauty, saw the loveliness of Its Face
and at once went raving mad;
borrowed sugar from Love's lips
and tasting it at once began to speak.

One needs Thy Light
To see Thee (pp. 74–75).

Julian of Norwich: "We can never cease from mourning and weeping, seeking and longing, until we see him
clearly, face to his blessed face, for in that precious sight no
woe can remain, no well-being can be lacking" (p. 320).

Jacob Boehme: "O God, Fountain-source of love and mercy, I praise and glorify You in Your truth, and thank You in my heart that you offer me Your face once more and look on me, unworthy and wretched [as I am], with the eyes of Your mercy, and give me again a beam of comfort so that my soul can hope on You. [. . .] The dry place of the heart and soul You water with Your rain, and give them the water of Your mercy" (p. 84).

Heart/emptying of images

The location of the first text in this approach may need some clarification. We have opted to put this text here because we see the image of Mary which John Cassian develops to be centered in his phrases, "that astonished gaze at His ungraspable nature" and, "It will be such a union that our breathing and our thinking and our talking will be 'God.' " For us, the images spring from an illumined heart which is reduced to the absence of any image but the one word "God." There are images involved, certainly, but there is a sense of the frailty of these images and an appeal to the "ungraspable nature" of God.

John Cassian: "To cling always to God and to the things of God—this must be our major effort, this must be the road that the heart follows unswervingly. Any diversion, however impressive, must be regarded as secondary, low-grade, and certainly dangerous. Martha and Mary provide a most beautiful scriptural model of this outlook and of this mode of activity. In looking after the Lord and His disciples Martha did a very holy service. Mary, however, was intent on the spiritual teaching of Jesus and she stayed by His feet, which she kissed and anointed with the oil of her good faith. [. . .] You will note that the Lord establishes as the prime good contemplation, that is, the gaze turned in the direction of the things of God. [. . .] In saying this the Lord locates the primary good not in activity, however praiseworthy, however abundantly fruitful, but in the truly simple and unified contemplation of [. . .] the beauty and knowledge of God" (pp. 42–43).

"Contemplation of God can be understood in more than one fashion. For God is not solely known by way of that astonished gaze at His ungraspable nature, something hidden thus far in the hope that comes with what has been promised us. He can also be sensed in the magnificence of creation, in the spectacle of His justice, and in the help He extends each day to the running of the world" (p. 50).

"As God loves us with a love that is true and pure, a love that never breaks, we too will be joined to Him in a never-ending unshakable love, and it will be such a union that our breathing and our thinking and our talking will be 'God' " (pp. 129–30).

✓   *The Cloud of Unknowing:* "Lift up your heart to God with a humble impulse of love; and have himself as your aim, not any of his goods. Take care that you avoid thinking of anything but himself, so that there is nothing for your reason or your will to work on except himself. [. . .] This is the work of the soul that pleases God most. [. . .] Labor in [this exercise] until you experience the desire. For when you first begin to undertake it, all that you find is a darkness, a sort of cloud of unknowing; you cannot tell what it is, except that you experience a simple reaching out to God. This darkness and cloud is always between you and your God, no matter what you do, and it prevents you from seeing him clearly by the light of understanding in your reason, and

from experiencing him in sweetness of love in your affection" (pp. 119–21).

"Now all rational creatures, angels and men alike, have
in them, each one individually, one chief working power
which is called a knowing power, and another chief working
power called a loving power; and of these two powers, God,
who is the maker of them, is always incomprehensible to the
first, the knowing power. But to the second, which is the
loving power, he is entirely comprehensible. . ." (p. 123).

Hadewijch:
Through desires of unquiet love
The soul can win no repose,
And through desires of strong love
It loses repose and inner quiet.
So it drowns in sublime Love,
And so it finds its unattainable desire nearby;
For anyone in misery cannot find contentment
Unless desire can be fulfilled;
For desire comes from such a lofty nature,
It cannot be at rest in any small thing.
Love flees, and desire follows hard after,
And never finds a resting place.
It cannot conquer sublimity;
What Love herself is must remain out of its reach
    (p. 338).

Rufus M. Jones (*Quaker Spirituality***):** "When I was too
young to have any religion of my own [. . .] we never began a
day without 'a family gathering' at which mother read a
chapter of the Bible, after which there would follow a
weighty silence. These silences, during which all the children of our family were hushed with a kind of awe, were

very important features of my spiritual development. There was work inside and outside the house waiting to be done, and yet we sat there hushed and quiet, doing nothing. I very quickly discovered that something *real* was taking place. We were feeling our way down to that place from which living words come" (p. 263).

George Herbert: "Come Lord, my head doth burn, my heart is sick, / While thou dost ever, ever stay: / Thy long deferrings wound me to the quick, / my spirit gaspeth night and day. / Oh show thyself to me, / Or take me up to thee!" (p. 227)

Mind/imaging

Several texts in this section deserve a word of explanation about their references to both understanding and feeling. Why do they deserve to be placed under this approach? The first text has its center in the author's "cleaving in full understanding" rather than his "cleaving in love." His concern is the divine light (illumination) which shows us the way of light and places us in the light of God. The second text, that of Teresa of Avila, could be read as referring to the illumination of the heart. Indeed, she says, the "important thing is not to think much but to love much." Yet Teresa seems to understand love in a quite rational manner! It is not the heart which makes value decisions for God, it is "strong determination" based in the end on an intellectual vision. Note her use of this phrase in the next quotation. For these reasons we have placed these texts under this approach.

Abraham Isaac Kook: "In place of the presumptuous and vain preoccupation with the divine *essence*, the human heart will be oriented to concern itself with pure morality, and the heroism for higher things, which emanate as flashes from the divine light and are at all times connected with its source, showing man the way of life and placing him in the light of God" (p. 265).

"The inner enlightenment that wells up forcefully within the person, and the enlightenment from without, the rational, that derives from the knowledge of the world and of reality, both contribute to building the human spirit. They perfect one's understanding and will, and they function jointly, even when a person is not conscious of it" (p. 206).

"One must always cleanse one's thoughts about God to make sure they are free of the dross of deceptive fantasies, of groundless fear, of evil inclinations, of wants and deficiencies. Then is the soul illuminated by the divine light, through cleaving in love and full understanding to Him who is the life of all life; and all feelings, all ideas and all actions, thus become refined. The attachment to God in feeling will have its effect in directing life on an upright path to the extent that this basic principle is operative in the soul, in a state of purity" (p. 261).

Teresa of Avila: "In order to profit by this path and ascend to the dwelling places we desire, the important thing is not to think much but to love much; and so to do that which best stirs you to love. Perhaps we don't know what love is. I wouldn't be very much surprised, because it doesn't consist in great delight but in desiring with strong determination to please God in everything, in striving, insofar as possible, not to offend Him, and in asking Him for the advancement of the honor and glory of His Son and the increase of the Catholic Church" (p. 70).

Nicodemos of the Holy Mountain: "According to the opinion of the theologians, the mind and God are a type one to another, as the mind who loves rises to God who is loved. The mind rises to God through contemplation of his divine perfections, while the beloved God condescends from his height toward the mind that loves him, uniting himself with it, and filling it with grace and deifying it. Thus, in his ascent of God the blessed and supernatural union of God and mind is accomplished: the lover with the beloved; the prototype with the image, or to put it simply, the Creator who is infinitely removed with the infinitely removed by nature creature" (p. 217).

Teresa of Avila: "But that which comes to pass in the union of the spiritual marriage is very different. The Lord appears in this center of the soul, not in an imaginative vision but in an intellectual one, although more delicate than those mentioned, as He appeared to the apostles without entering through the door when He said to them *pax vobis* [peace be with you]. What God communicates here to the soul in an instant is a secret so great and a favor so sublime—and the delight the soul experiences so extreme—that I don't know what to compare it to. I can only say that the Lord wishes to reveal for that moment, in a more sublime manner than through any spiritual vision or taste, the glory of heaven" (p. 178).

Robert Bellarmine: "Lift up your mind, my soul, to your exemplar and consider that the whole excellence of an image lies in its similarity to its exemplar. [. . .] Your exemplar, O soul, is God—infinite beauty, 'light, and in him there is no darkness' (1 Jn 1:5), at whose beauty the sun and moon gaze in awe. So that you may more easily imitate the beauty of such an exemplar and desire to mirror it and achieve this

by every means (in this lie all your perfection, all your useful-
ness, all your honor, all your joy, all your rest, and all your
good), consider that the beauty of God your exemplar consists in wisdom and holiness" (pp. 60–61).

Abraham Isaac Kook: "But it is precisely when the
lights are in convulsion, and the vessels that have housed
them seem about to break, that there is need to proclaim that
indeed the letters, the words, the actions, are not the essence
of the light, but they are vessels, the organs of a living body,
which bears within itself a soul. But alas for anyone who
denies them even the role of vessels. Whoever denies the
holiness of the letters, the words, the actions and the forms
within their own domain, will render himself speechless,
without utterance, without any inner conceptual image, and
altogether without the power to act, flooded by various
forces that will disturb him altogether, body and soul.

"Raise up religion, elevate thought, acclaim the real life,
lived according to the conceptual forms and the practical
actions in which the imagination has robed the higher light"
(p. 269).

Johann Arndt: "In Genesis 29:17–25 we read that Jacob
wishes to have the woman Rachel as his beautiful wife, but
he had to take Leah first. Leah was physically ugly; Rachel
was pretty and beautiful. Therefore, if you wish to have the
beautiful Rachel, that is, if your soul is to be the wife of
Jacob, that is, of Christ, you must first take to yourself Leah,
that is, you must not be pleasing to yourself, you must be
hateful to yourself, ugly, you must hate yourself and deny
yourself" (p. 72).

"The image of God in man is that conformity with God
in which the likeness of the invisible God is characteristically

and vitally published and shines forth, namely, as a likeness of goodness, righteousness, holiness, immortality, wisdom, mercy, might, power and faith, and so forth. These characteristics, since they are essentially and infinitely together in God, God himself wishes to express in man as a living portrait and image" (p. 247).

Beginning of Wisdom (*Safed Spirituality*): "So it is with Torah scholars who are separated from their wives all week long because of their 'marital' duty to the King's daughter, that is, the Torah.[1] It is proper for them to make haste in their desire for the Torah, for through its study they cleave to the life of the upper realm as well as to the Shekhinah. She comes and pours forth divine abundance upon them from the Holy Spirit" (p. 139).

Catherine of Siena: "A soul rises up, restless with tremendous desire for God's honor and the salvation of souls. She has for some time exercised herself in virtue and has become accustomed to dwelling in the cell of self-knowledge in order to know better God's goodness toward her, since upon knowledge follows love. And loving, she seeks to pursue truth and clothe herself in it. But there is no way she can so savor and be enlightened by this truth as in continual humble prayer, grounded in the knowledge of herself and God" (p. 25).

Mind/emptying of images

Gregory Palamas: "Similarly, beyond the stripping away of beings, or rather after the cessation [of our perceiv-

---

1. Two words occur in this text which may be unfamiliar: "Torah" is the first of the three divisions of the Hebrew scriptures and includes the first five books of the Old Testament; "Shekhinah" is the Presence of God or its manifestation.

ing or thinking of them] accomplished not only in words, but in reality, there remains an unknowing which is beyond knowledge; though indeed a darkness, it is yet beyond radiance, and, as the great Denys says, it is in this dazzling darkness that the divine things are given to the saints" (p. 36).

☑ **William Law:** "Before or without nature, the Deity is an entire hidden, shut up, unknown, and unknowable abyss. For nature is the only ground or beginning of something; there is neither this nor that, no ground for conception, no possibility of distinction or difference; there cannot be a creature to think, nor anything to be thought upon until nature is in existence. For all the properties of sensibility and sensible life, every mode and manner of existence, all seeing, hearing, tasting, smelling, feeling, all inclinations, passions, and sensations of joy, sorrow, pain, pleasure, etc., are not in God but in nature. And therefore, God is not knowable, not a thought can begin about Him till He manifests Himself in and through and by the existence of nature, that is, till there is something that can be seen, understood, distinguished, felt, etc." (p. 418).

Menahem Nahum of Chernobyl: "Purify your mind and thought from thinking too many different thoughts. You have only to think about one thing: serving God in joy. The word *Be-SiMHaH* ('in joy') has the same letters as *MaHaSha-BaH* ('thought'); all thoughts that come to you should be included in this single one. Of this Scripture speaks in 'Many are the thoughts in a person's mind, but it is the counsel of the Lord that will stand' (Prov 19:21). Understand this.

"Our rabbis say: 'Sanctify yourself within the realm of that which is permitted.' In the moment of sexual union turn your thoughts to the sake of heaven" (p. 31).

William Law: "The greater any man's mind, the more

he knows of God and himself, the more will he be disposed to prostrate himself before God in all the humblest acts and expressions of repentance" (p. 343).

✓   **Meister Eckhart (*Essential Sermons*):** "When I preach, I am accustomed to speak about detachment, and that a man should be free of himself and of all things; second, that a man should be formed again into that simple good which is God; third, that he should reflect on the great nobility with which God has endowed his soul, so that in this way he may come to wonder at God; fourth, about the purity of the divine nature, for the brightness of the divine nature is beyond words. God is a word, a word unspoken" (p. 203).

John of the Cross: "Poor, abandoned, and unsupported by any of the apprehensions of my soul (in the darkness of my intellect, the distress of my will, and in the affliction and anguish of my memory), left to darkness in pure faith, which is a dark night [. . .] I went out from myself. That is, I departed from my low manner of understanding, and my feeble way of loving, and my poor and limited method of finding satisfaction in God. I did this unhindered by either the flesh or the devil.

"This was great happiness and a sheer grace for me, because through the annihilation and calming of my faculties, passions, appetites, and affection, but which my experience and satisfaction in God was base, I went out from my human operation and way of acting to God's operation and way of acting" (p. 200).

> To come to the knowledge of all
>   desire the knowledge of nothing.
> [. . .]
> To come to the knowledge you have not

you must go by a way in which you know not.
[. . .]
When you turn toward something you cease to cast
    yourself upon the all.
For to go from the all to the all
    you must deny yourself of all in all.
And when you come to the possession of the all
    you must possess it without wanting anything.
Because if you desire to have something in all
    your treasure in God is not purely your all
    (pp. 78–79).

Johannes Tauler: "Whoever arrives here has discovered what he has been searching for far and wide. His spirit will be led into a hidden desert far beyond his natural faculties. Words cannot describe it, for it is the unfathomable darkness where the divine Goodness reigns above all distinctions. And the soul is led further, into the oneness of God's simple unity, so that it loses the ability to draw any distinctions between the object and its own emotions. For in this unity all multiplicity is lost; it is the unity which unifies multiplicity. [. . .]

"This state is called and indeed is an unfathomable darkness, and yet it is the essential light. It is and is said to be an incomprehensible and solitary wilderness, for no one can find his way there, for it is above all ways, above all modes and manners.

"This 'darkness' is to be understood in such a way: It is a light inaccessible to created reason, far beyond its comprehension. It is a wilderness because no natural path leads to it. In this wilderness the spirit is raised above itself, above all its powers of comprehension and understanding, and the soul now drinks from the very spring, from the true and essential source" (p. 59).

"Thus we behold and perceive, by means of the created light, the divine, uncreated One. All this comes to us first in a veiled manner, for our faculties cannot come within a thousand miles of this depth of the soul. The breadth which opens up here has neither form nor image nor any other mode or manner; nor are there any concepts of space. For it is an unfathomable abyss, poised in itself, unplumbed, ebbing and flowing like the sea. As one is immersed in it, it seems still and void; yet in an instant it wells up as if it would engulf all things. One sinks into this abyss, and in it is God's own dwelling-place, more real than in Heaven and in all His creatures. Whoever finds his way there would truly find God, and himself one with God, for God would never part from it again. God would be present to him, and here eternity would be tasted and savored, for there exists no past or future" (p. 147).

3. Love of God and Neighbor

T he second question asks: "What is the relationship between the love of God and the love of neighbor?" In what precise ways are the love of God and the love of neighbor bound together? Are they inextricably interwoven? Can they be separated? Is one of more importance than the other? Is one prior to the other? Is one possible without the other? Are they of different "orders"—that is, does one love the neighbor directly and God only indirectly?

The question may also be understood to inquire about God's love for the neighbor as well as our love for the neighbor. Do we discover who is our neighbor by asking who it is that God loves? Does God's love for our neighbor put demands on us? Who is our neighbor? Are family and friends *more* our neighbor than those at a distance?

As with the other questions, your interpretation of the question as well as your response is of great importance. In your life you have sorted out your answer in action and words; and your answer reflects your understanding of the question and its importance for the spiritual life. Try now to be as full as you can in your answer to the question: "What is the relationship between the love of God and the love of neighbor?" Think back over your life—has your answer always been the same as it is today? What are the turning points in your understanding of this question? How does it color your relationship to family and friends, to strangers and enemies? Take time to answer the question as fully as you can; cherish your own answers and your own starting points in the conversation.

Now go to the block of texts which represent the approach most comfortable for you. Find there a companion in the quest with whom you are at home; chew over what the quote means, what thoughts and feelings it arouses in you. Do not expect to find that approach dictates content. For example, in the first set of quotations authors come to quite different understandings of the relationship between the love of God and the love of neighbor. For some, any love of neighbor is love of God—whether we know it or not. For others, the love of God is so sublime that we hardly see, as it were, the neighbor we serve. Now, with attention and openness of spirit, enter into conversation with the texts; let them speak to you.

Heart/imaging

Fakhruddin ʿIraqi: "Love is the lover's essence, nor could this essence cease to be, however his attachment may flit from beloved to beloved.

> Shift, transfer your heart where you will—
> Love belongs but to the First Beloved.

"Love where you may, you will have loved Him; turn your face whatever way, it turns toward Him—even if you know it not."

"It is not so much wrong as impossible to love other than Him, for whatever we love (aside from that love which springs from the very essence of the love, the cause of which

is unknown), we love either for its beauty, or its goodness—
and both of these belong to Him alone."

> The beauty of each lovely boy
>   each comely girl
> derives from His—
>   on loan (p. 85).

Francis de Sales: "Try interrupting the meditations of
someone who is very attached to her spiritual exercises and
you will see her upset, flustered, taken aback. A person who
has this true freedom will leave her prayer, unruffled,
gracious toward the person who has unexpectedly disturbed
her, for to her it's all the same—serving God by meditating
or serving Him by responding to her neighbor. Both are the
will of God, but helping the neighbor is necessary at that
particular moment" (pp. 138–39).

Catherine of Siena: "Just so, it is impossible to fulfill
the law concerning [love for] me, God eternal, apart from the
[law concerning love for] your neighbors. These are the two
feet of affection on which you must follow the commandments and counsels" (p. 165).

"It is an easy matter, for nothing is as easy and delightful as love. And what I ask of you is nothing other than love
and affection for me and for your neighbors. This can be
done at any time, any place, and in any state of life by loving
and keeping all things for the praise and glory of my name.
"You know (for I have told you) that some deluded
souls clothe themselves in selfish love of themselves rather
than walk in the light. They love and possess creatures apart
from me, and so they pass through this life tormented, becoming insupportable even to themselves" (p. 110).

"And though [just souls] are all joined in the bond of charity, they know a special kind of sharing with those whom they loved most closely with a special love in the world, a love through which they grew in grace and virtue. They helped each other proclaim the glory and praise of my name in themselves and in their neighbors. So now in everlasting life they have not lost that love; no, they still love and share with each other even more closely and fully, adding their love to the good of all" (p. 83).

"These are the true workers. They till their souls well, uprooting every selfish love, cultivating the soil of their love in me. They feed and tend the growth of the seed of grace that they received in holy baptism. And as they till their own vineyards, so they till their neighbors' as well, for they cannot do the one without the other. You already know that every evil as well as every good is done by means of your neighbors" (p. 62).

"For in charity their neighbors find me, but in their own pleasure, where they are seeking me, they will be deprived of me" (p. 131).

Symeon the New Theologian: "As soon as I called to mind the beauty of undefiled love, its light suddenly appeared in my heart. I have been ravished with its delight and have ceased to perceive outward things; I have lost all sense of this life and have forgotten the things that are at hand. Yet again—I am at a loss how to say it—it has removed far from me and has left me to lament my own weakness. O all-desirable love, how happy is he who has embraced you, for he will no longer have a passionate desire to embrace any earthly beauty! Happy is he who is moved by divine love to cling to you! He will deny the whole world, yet as he associates with all men he will be wholly untainted. Happy is he who caresses your beauty and with infinite desire delights therein. [. . .] In spirit and soul he will rejoice, because you are the ineffable joy" (p. 43).

"Learn in how awesome a manner our earthly [being] is re-created, and how those men live who have consented to believe in Christ crucified, that is, those who imitate His obedience and self-abasement and desire to turn from evil to good. [. . .] While they live and move among all men they are by no means defiled by their converse with others. When they do well to those who come to them they suffer no loss of what is good, but as they impart to others they receive more mercy than they give. Rather, as they love others they become like Him who is the Lover of mankind" (p. 207).

John Wesley: "Suffer me to exclude none, O Lord, from my charity, who are the objects of your mercy; but let me treat all my neighbors with that tender love which is due to your servants and to your children. [. . .] You have redeemed them with an inestimable price; assisted by your Holy Spirit, therefore, I will endeavor to recover them from a state of destruction; that thus adorning your holy Gospel, by doing good according to my power, I may at last be received into the endearments of your eternal love" (p. 83).

"And loving God he loves his neighbor as himself; he loves every man as his own soul. He loves his enemies, yea, and the enemies of God" (p. 304).

Francisco de Osuna: "Do not think that the people you observe who are tearful and sad with the world, hungry, ill-clothed, ravaged by sleeplessness, scorned and persecuted, their eyes sunken, colorless, little more than skin and bone, at war with the licentious, are content with their hardship. How could you presume them satisfied when you know how difficult life is even if we have our own way! Undoubtedly these people would quickly weaken if Our Lord God did not welcome them with open arms and deeper happiness and sweeter consolation than even the mother shows when her little child seeks refuge from pain in her embrace. The mother hugs her child, then, pressing him to her breast, quells his hunger, and with her face close, his groaning, tears, and fear subside.

"We read that Our Lord God is so anxious for our love that he acted in the same way when the sinner arrived from a distant land [. . .]" (p. 46).

Heart/emptying of images

The first approach is characterized by rich imagery as a path to illumination of the heart. In the present approach there is characteristically an emptying of images, although the goal is the same, namely, the illumination of the heart. Some of the texts which follow clearly fit in this category; others do not seem to fit so clearly because they use images to make their point. For example, in the last text Hadewijch says: "Because Love consoles the young lovers anew, they fancy they are fully free." There is an image here, but there is also at root a distrust of the image—the young lovers *wrongly* fancy they are fully free—which has led us to assign this text to the heart/emptying of images approach.

Augustine: "Therefore once for all this short command is given to you: 'Love and do what you will.' If you keep silent, keep silent by love; if you speak, speak by love; if you correct, correct by love; if you pardon, pardon by love: let love be rooted in you, and from the root nothing but good can grow" (p. 305).

"What then do I love when I love my God? Who is He above the summit of my soul? Through this very soul of mine I shall ascend to Him. I shall go beyond my life-force by which I cling to the body and fill its frame with life" (p. 127).

John Cassian: "And these will be the signs of God being all that we love and all that we want. He will be all that we are zealous for, all that we strive for. He will be all that we think about, all our living, all that we talk about, our very breath. And that union of Father and Son, of Son and Father, will fill our senses and our minds. As God loves us with a love that is true and pure, a love that never breaks, we too will be joined to Him in a never-ending unshakable love, and it will be such a union that our breathing and our thinking and our talking will be 'God' " (pp. 129–130).

Rufus M. Jones: "When my sorrow was at its most acute stage [for the death of my son] I was walking along a great city highway [Birmingham], when suddenly I saw a little child come out of a great gate, which swung to and fastened behind her. She wanted to go to her home behind the gate, but it would not open. She pounded in vain with her little fist. She rattled the gate. Then she wailed as though her heart would break. The cry brought the mother. She caught the child in her arms and kissed away the tears. 'Didn't you know I would come? It is all right now.' All of a sudden I saw with my spirit that there was love behind my shut gate.
"Yes, 'Where there is so much love *there must be* more' " (p. 274).

The Cloud of Unknowing: "In the same way, it would be very inappropriate and a great hindrance to a man who ought to be working in this darkness and in this cloud of unknowing, with an affective impulse of love to God for himself alone, to permit any thought or any meditation on God's wonderful gifts, kindness or his work in any of his creatures, bodily or spiritual, to rise up in his mind so as to press between him and his God, even if they should be very holy thoughts, and give him great happiness and consolation.

"This is the reason why I bid you put down any such clear and insinuating thought, and cover it up with a thick cloud of forgetting, no matter how holy it might be, and no matter how well it might promise to help you in your endeavor. Because it is love alone that can reach God in this life, and not knowing" (pp. 138–39).

Angelus Silesius:
Man, creatures love you so, it's you they are pressing toward;
Hastening to come to you, thus to attain their God
(p. 52).

The Pursuit of Wisdom: "And now a manner of homeliness begins to grow up between God and a man's soul, and a certain kindling of love; so much so that a man is oftentimes aware that he is being visited by God and is also greatly comforted by his coming. Lia was first aware of this homeliness and this kindling of love when, after Levi was born, she cried out with great joy and said, 'Now my husband will be joined to me.' The true husband of our soul is God. And we are truly joined to him when we draw near to him in hope and steadfast love" (pp. 24–25).

Ephrem the Syrian: "One drunk on wine is more tolerable than one drunk on hateful love" (p. 264).

Hadewijch:
Because Love consoles the young lovers anew,
They fancy then they are fully free;
    So they are as if at court,
And live well satisfied with themselves
And fancy they have fought in the joust
    With the fullest praise.
      If reason then disillusions them,
      And holds up before them the work
They have to do,
    With a change of mood
    They experience fear
And lose their first boldness (p. 167).

    Love conquers all things:
May she help me to conquer in my turn!
    And may she who knows every need
Grant that I may learn
    How hard it is for me
    (Had I the chance)
To wait for the fruition of Love:
    Cruel reason,
    Which helps against it,
Introduces confusion in my mental powers (p. 169).

Mind/imaging

Augustine: "We should not be anxious about the question of how much love we should give to our brother and how much to God. The answer is: to God far more than to ourselves, and to our brother as much as ourselves; the more we love God the more we love ourselves. We love God and our neighbor from one and the same love, but we love God for God's sake, and we love ourselves and our neighbor for God's sake" (pp. 328–29).

Teresa of Avila: "We cannot know whether or not we love God, although there are strong indications for recognizing that we do love Him; but we can know whether we love our neighbor. And be certain that the more advanced you see you are in love for your neighbor the more advanced you will be in the love of God, for the love His Majesty has for us is so great that to repay us for our love of neighbor He will in a thousand ways increase the love we have for Him" (p. 100).

"If we fail in love of neighbor we are lost. May it please the Lord that this will never be so; for if you do not fail, I tell you that you shall receive from His Majesty the union that was mentioned. When you see yourselves lacking in this love, even though you have devotion and gratifying experiences that make you think you have reached this stage, and you experience some little suspension in the prayer of quiet (for to some it then appears that everything has been accomplished), believe me, you have not reached union. And beg our Lord to give you this perfect love of neighbor" (p. 102).

"Let us love the one who offends us since this great God has not ceased to love us even though we have offended Him very much. Thus the Lord is right in wanting all to pardon the wrongs done to them" (p. 164).

Johann Arndt: "Love is the whole heart of man and the most noble force. It is to be given to God alone as the noblest and highest Good.

"It is the greatest foolishness to love that which cannot love us in return. The temporal, weak, dead thing has no love for us and, therefore, it is useless for us to love it. Much more, we are with our hearts to love God above all creatures, for he loves us so much that he created us for eternal life, redeemed us, and made us holy.

"It is natural that each person should love that which he is like. Therefore, God created you to his image and likeness so that you might love him and your neighbor" (p. 97).

"The love of a good conscience is the love of neighbor. The love of God and the love of neighbor are one thing and must not be divided. The true divine love cannot be better noted or proven than in the love of neighbor" (p. 126).

"Therefore, our brother is a test for us, established by the love of God, that is, God wishes to test us in our neighbor [to see] whether our love is righteous before him. God does not need our service in the slightest way, but our neighbor does" (p. 130).

Jacob Boehme: "Let such a man merely do this thing in a (sensual) consideration and look at the whole course of his life, and hold it up against the Ten Commandments of God and against the love of the Gospel that asks him to love his neighbor as he loves himself, so that he be a child of grace only in Christ's love" (p. 66).

Robert Bellarmine: "If you wish to share this glory, you must first conform your body to the body of Christ's humility. Then you must follow his footsteps. [. . .] Christ has two footsteps; if you step out of them, you have lost the way and will never reach your fatherland; do not do evil but suffer it, and what follows from this, do good without expecting good here below. It all comes down to this: You must love your neighbor for God's sake with the true and pure love of friendship and not out of gain, gratuitously and not for the sake of human reward, content with a reward from God which surpasses all measure" (pp. 147–48).

"Love comes not from the world but from God, as the beloved disciple says in his Letter (1 Jn 4:7). From love as from a divine and heavenly tree there spring forth bright flowers fragrant with holy thoughts, green leaves useful for the salvation of the nations, and the fruits of good works which glorify God, help the neighbor, gather merit, and remain unto eternal life" (p. 82).

Menachem Nahum of Chernobyl: "It is proper that man should stand in awe of God [not only when His might is revealed, but] also when He gives him goodness and blessing. This is 'the great and awesome God' (Deut 7:21). This is also 'the love of God all the day' (Ps 52:3); it too should call forth awe. Such is not the way of the wicked: when they see the countenance of the Lord shining on them they lose their fear. In this way they cause trouble and bring about judgment" (p. 99).

"According to the symbols of the Kabbalah, Abraham represents the attribute of divine love (*hesed*) and the right hand of God. [. . .] The Ba'al Shem was said to have taught that he had come into the world only for the sake of love: for the love of God, the love of Israel, and the love of Torah. No Hasidic teacher would have argued with the definition of his role. No doubt that it was in many cases the masters' unusual warmth and love for their disciples, including a loving acceptance of even the most seemingly wanting of them, that gave them their large following. For *hasidim* this love was completely natural, surely nothing other than a continuation of that love which father Abraham had shown to strangers as he welcomed them into his ever-open tent, fed them, and spoke to them of the greatness of the Lord" (p. 104).

"It sometimes happens that a person feels himself to be in a fallen state, overtaken by the negative side of his own inner qualities, especially by improper love in the form of sexual desire. This may even happen when the desired sexual act is a permitted one. Such a person should know that heaven desires to uplift him, using his own natural emotions in order to open his heart to the love of God, so that he may receive Torah as gift" (p. 117).

"The opposite is true of one whose heart remains uncircumcised. Then the evil side of each of these qualities comes to reside in the foreskin of his flesh. All of such a person's desires are turned to sexual defilement. [. . .]
"For this reason the Talmud tells us that in the days of the early rabbis a young man would go off to a house of study for several years immediately following his marriage. This was in order to break down desire by means of circumcising the heart, setting their moral lives aright and especially uplifting any fallen love through the study of Torah" (pp. 120–21).

Mind/emptying of images

William Law: "Oh Sir! Would you know the blessing of all blessings? It is this God of love dwelling in your soul and killing every root of bitterness which is the pain and torment of every earthly, selfish love. For all wants are satisfied, all disorders of nature are removed, no life is any longer a burden, every day is a day of peace, everything you meet becomes a help to you because everything you see or do is all done in the sweet, gentle element of love. For as love has no by-ends, will nothing but its own increase, so everything is as oil to its flame" (pp. 358–59).

Meister Eckhart: "By the fact that God is called love absolutely, the first thing demonstrated is his purest and most complete simplicity, and from this his priority over all things. His existence is simple existence [. . .]; he is something eternal and not subject to time. Those wishing to be united with him must come to be outside time" (p. 212).

"God is and is said to be love principally because he is the one whom everything that can love loves and seeks. Again, he alone is the one who is love and sought by all and in all. Also, everything that exists and can exist subsists in seeking and loving him. Again, it is he in whom everything that is unpleasant, contrary, sad, or nonexistent is sweet and beautiful. Without him anything pleasant is disagreeable and nonexistent. Furthermore, God is love because he is totally lovable and totally love" (p. 213).

Augustine: "This is what you should think, if you wish to see God: 'God is Love.' What face has love? What form has it? What height? What feet? What hands? No one can say. Yet it has feet, for they lead to the Church; it has hands, for they care for the poor; it has eyes, for through them the needy one is known" (pp. 305–6).

Johannes Tauler: "Beloved! You do not know what love is. You believe you have found it, because you experience powerful emotions, and feel joy and delight; but this is not love at all. This is not how love behaves. When we love we are aflame, desiring God, lacking God, feeling forsaken by God, in constant torment, yet content to be tormented;

consumed by the fire of our thirst for God, and yet, through it all, content. This is love, quite different from what you imagined it to be; it is the lantern ignited" (p. 125).

William Law: "For the life of the creature, whilst only creaturely and possessing nothing but itself, is Hell; that is, it is all pain and want and distress. Now nothing in the nature of the thing can make the least alteration in this creaturely life, nothing can help it to be in light and love, in peace and goodness, but the union of God with it, and the life of God working in it, because nothing but God is life, and love, and heavenly goodness. And therefore, where the life of God is not become the life and goodness of the creature, there the creature cannot have the least degree of goodness in it" (p. 402).

Maximus Confessor: "1. Love is a good disposition of the soul by which one prefers no being to the knowledge of God. It is impossible to reach the habit of this love if one has any attachment to earthly things.
"2. Love is begotten of detachment, detachment of hope in God, hope of patient endurance and long-suffering, these of general self-mastery, self-mastery of fear of God, and fear of faith in the Lord.
"10. When in the full ardor of its love for God the mind goes out of itself, then it has no perception at all either of itself or of any creatures. For once illumined by the divine and infinite light, it remains insensible to anything that is made by him, just as the physical eye has no sensation of the stars when the sun has risen" (p. 36).

Gregory Palamas: "Impassibility does not consist in mortifying the passionate part of the soul, but in removing it from evil to good, and directing its energies towards divine things. [. . .] It is not thus the man who has killed the passionate part of his soul who has the preeminence, for such a one would have no momentum or activity to acquire a divine state and right dispositions and relationship with God; but rather, the prize goes to him who has put that part of his soul under subjection, so that by its obedience to the mind, which is by nature appointed to rule, it may ever tend towards God, as is right, by the uninterrupted remembrance of Him. Thanks to this remembrance, he will come to possess a divine disposition, and cause the soul to progress towards the highest state of all, the love of God. Through this love, he will accomplish the commandments of Him whom he loves, in accord with the Scriptures, and will put into practice and acquire a pure and perfect love for his neighbor, something that cannot exist without impassibility" (pp. 54–55).

4. Prayer

T he third question—"What is prayer?"—inquires about prayer in a variety of ways: Where and when do you best pray? What is the importance of prayer? What is the result or effect of prayer? As prayer is so central to the spiritual life it may be helpful to spend extra time in this chapter and to return to it from time to time. One of the key polarities we emphasize is shown here in a particular way. Techniques of meditation, the ways you pray, may stress either images or the emptying of images. We encourage you to be attentive not only to your preferred type and its opposite, but to spend time with all four quadrants of the circle. You will learn much about prayer and about your own spiritual life.

First, though, we acknowledge that for many the topic of prayer is very threatening. Some people are unsure whether or not they *ever* pray. Oh, they say "prayers" but do they really pray? Please do not let any sense of anxiety creep into your mind or heart at this point. It is quite likely that you will find in the quotes which follow that you do indeed pray. However, it may be that you pray without images—quickly, perhaps, and almost by instinct rather than with words. Or it may be that you have to acknowledge, with sorrow, that you have not dedicated yourself very much to prayer. If that is the case, with the psalmist, David, say: "Now, I begin!" But do not judge yourself too harshly. Paul is wonderfully consoling in this regard. "The Spirit too comes to help us in our weakness. For when we cannot choose words in order to pray properly, the Spirit expresses our plea in a way that could never be put into words, and God who knows everything in our hearts knows perfectly well what the Spirit means" (Rom 8:26–27).

Prayer is such a taken-for-granted part of the spiritual life, that changes in the life of prayer may go unremarked and occur without adequate reflection. As you answer these questions about prayer, be attentive to the nature and role of prayer at various points in your spiritual journey. It may surprise you that your understanding and practice of prayer have developed so much over the years. Once again we encourage you to write with the confidence that what you have to say is worthwhile. No negative self-talk! We have all known failure in prayer; we have all neglected to pray. Yet even our faltering attempts may represent growth over the years.

In the quotes that follow you will glimpse some of the richness and complexity of prayer. You will also note the distinctiveness of the four approaches to the spiritual life. It is no longer enough to define prayer as the lifting up of the *mind and heart* to God: mind and heart each bring to bear a certain dimension of the self, as does our preference either for images or emptying of images.

Heart/imaging

Julian of Norwich: "The whole reason why we pray is to be united into the vision and contemplation of [the one] to whom we pray, wonderfully rejoicing with reverent fear" (p. 254).

"Prayer is a right understanding of that fullness of joy which is to come, with true longing and trust. The savoring or seeing of our bliss, to which we are ordained, by nature makes us to long; true understanding and love, with a sweet recollection in our savior, by grace makes us to trust" (p. 252).

"And so he teaches us to pray and to have firm trust that we shall have it; for he beholds us in love, and wants to make us partners in his good will and work. And so he moves us to pray for what it pleases him to do, and for this prayer and good desire which come to us by his gift he will repay us, and give us eternal reward. And this was revealed to me when he said: If you beseech it" (p. 253).

"Pray wholeheartedly, though you may feel nothing, though you may see nothing, yes, though you think that you could not, for in dryness and in barrenness, in sickness and in weakness, then is your prayer most pleasing to me, though you think it almost tasteless to you. And so is all your living prayer in my sight" (p. 249).

Catherine of Siena: "Perfect prayer is achieved not with many words but with loving desire" (p. 126).
"Courageously, then, should the soul spur herself on with prayer as her mother" (p. 127).

John Eudes: "This holy exercise of prayer [. . .] is more essential for a Christian who wants to live a Christian life than are the earth which supports us, the air which we breathe, the bread which sustains us and the heart which beats in our breast necessary to us for human life" (p. 313).

"There [in prayer] God teaches us experientially that true delight and perfect happiness are found in God and that a hundred, even a thousand years of the false pleasures of the world do not equal one moment of the authentic delights that God allows those souls to taste, whose greatest joy is to commune with him through holy prayer" (p. 314).

Francis de Sales: "Once you have resolved to follow your affection, dearest daughter, don't waste your time during prayer trying to understand exactly what you are doing or how you are praying; for the best prayer is that which keeps us so occupied with God that we don't think about ourselves or about what we are doing" (p. 167).

"Your way of praying is good. Just be very faithful about staying near God, gently and quietly attentive to Him in your heart, sleeping in the arms of His providence, peacefully accepting His holy will; for all this pleases Him" (p. 151).

John Wesley:
Thy soul break out in strong desire
        The perfect bliss to prove!
Thy longing heart be all on fire
        To be dissolv'd in love! (p. 336).

I want a heart to pray,
        To pray and never cease,
Never to murmur at thy stay,
        Or wish my sufferings less
This blessing above all,
        Always to pray I want,
Out of the deep on thee to call,
        And never, never faint (p. 210).

Symeon the New Theologian: "For if you say that it is impossible daily to repent and to weep and shed tears, then how can you say that it is possible for men who are subject to corruption ever to attain to a humble mind, to rejoice at all times and to pray without ceasing (1 Thess 5:17), let alone attain a heart that is pure from all kinds of passions and evil thoughts so that one may see God" (p. 83).

"So I entered the place where I usually prayed and, mindful of the words of the holy man I began to say, 'Holy God.' At once I was so greatly moved to tears and loving desire for God that I would be unable to describe in words the joy and pure delight I then felt" (p. 200).

Francis of Assisi:
Almighty, eternal, just and merciful God,
grant us in our misery [the grace]
to do for You alone
what we know You want us to do
and always
to desire what pleases You.
Thus,
inwardly cleansed,
interiorly enlightened,
and inflamed by the fire of the Holy Spirit,
may we be able to follow
in the footprints of Your beloved Son,
our Lord Jesus Christ.
And,
by Your grace alone,
may we make our way to You (p. 13).

"The Devotion" (*Devotio Moderna*): "This we owe God: We should know him, fear him, worship him, love him, praise him, preach and bless him, exalt him, glorify him, magnify him, sanctify him, give thanks to him, submit ourselves and all our things to him, trust in him and obey, and resign ourselves to him. He who wishes to be seen by God should look upon him. In prayer give shape to one of these attitudes: modesty, weeping, affection, love, pleasantness, or wonder. No one can praise God from his heart unless God pleases him" (p. 214).

Francisco de Osuna: "Friendship and communion with God are possible in this life of exile. This friendship is not remote but more sure and more intimate than ever existed between brothers or even between mother and child" (p. 45).

"The second kind of prayer is that within our hearts, wherein we do not pronounce the words vocally with the mouth. We pray like this when our hearts speak alone with the Lord and we beseech him from within for everything we need. Greater favors usually are bestowed at such times when we commune alone with the Lord, as if in secret, so that no one hears us speaking as it were into his ear. David prayed in this manner when he said to God" 'Your servant has found his heart to pray to you' " (p. 345).

"God's greatest gift to his friend is himself, and man's greatest gift to God is himself" (p. 350).

Feeling/emptying of images

The author of *The Cloud of Unknowing:* "We must therefore pray in the height and the depth, the length and the breadth of our spirit; and not in many words but in a little word of one syllable. [. . .] And if we desire with all our intent to pray for the attainment of any good, let us cry either verbally or in thought or desire, using nothing else, nor any other word, but this word 'God' " (pp. 195–96).

John Ruusbroec: "Sometimes God gives such persons short flashes of spiritual insight, just like flashes of lightning in the sky. These are short flashes of singular resplendence which shine forth from out of a simple bareness. In an instant the spirit is raised above itself, but at once the light is past and the person comes to himself again" (p. 87).

John Cassian: "To keep the thought of God always in your mind you must cling totally to this formula for piety: 'Come to my help, O God; Lord, hurry to my rescue' (Ps 69:2). [. . .] This short verse is an indomitable wall for all those struggling against the onslaught of demons. It is an impenetrable breastplate and the sturdiest of shields. Whatever the disgust, the anguish, or the gloom in our thoughts, this verse keeps us from despairing of our salvation since it reveals to us the One to whom we call, the One who sees our struggles and who is never far from those who pray to Him" (pp. 132–33).

Jacopone da Todi:
Seeing his own sinfulness, man sighed disconsolately;
As he wept without cease, Compunction came to his
    side:
This was the moment for Penitence and her children
To enter his heart and take up their abode.
Confession spoke to them, but there was no way
In which man could make satisfaction.
[. . .]

Penitence sent Prayer to inform the Heavenly Court
Of man's plight, and his despair,

And how he was barred from making satisfaction.
'I cry out not to Reason but to Mercy;
She it is I choose as my advocate.
My offering is the tears of a bitter and contrite heart'
(p. 147).

Hadewijch: "Between God and the blissful soul that has become God with God, there reigns a spiritual charity. So whenever God reveals this spiritual charity to the soul, there rises within it a tender friendship (cf. Rom 8:28). That is, it feels within it how God is its friend before all pain, in all pain, yes, beyond all pain, in fidelity toward his Father. And this tender friendship gives rise to a sublime confidence. In this sublime confidence there rises a genuine sweetness. In this genuine sweetness rises a veritable joy. In this veritable joy there rises a divine clarity. Then the soul sees, and it sees nothing" (p. 111).

George Herbert:
When my devotions could not pierce
    Thy silent ears;
Then was my heart broken, as was my verse:
    My breast was full of fears
    And disorder (p. 197).

Thomas R. Kelly: "What is urged here are secret habits of unceasing orientation of the deeps of our being about the Inward Light, ways of conducting our inward life so that we are perpetually bowed in worship, while we are also very busy in the world of daily affairs. There is then no need for fret when faithfully turning to him, if he leads us but slowly into his secret chambers. If he gives us increasing steadiness in the deeper sense of his Presence, we can only quietly thank him. [. . .]

"To some at least he gives an amazing stayedness in him, a well-nigh unbroken life of humble quiet adoration in his Presence, in the depths of our being. Day and night, winter and summer, sunshine and shadow. He is here, the great Champion. And we are with him, held in his tenderness, quickened into quietness and peace. [. . .] Here is not ecstasy but serenity, unshakableness, firmness of life-orientation.

"There come times when [. . .] in holy hush we bow in Eternity, and know the divine Concern tenderly enwrapping us and all things within his persuading love. Here all human initiative has passed into acquiescence" (pp. 290, 293, 294).

Sharafuddin Maneri: "Anything at all should be considered as an idol, whether it be profitable or harmful, if fear or hope is associated with it, even though, in and of itself, it is not an idol. This is what Abraham, the Friend of God, meant when he said, 'Look at me! I cannot take any rest except with You; nor do I see anything but You; nor do I hope in anyone except you; nor do I fear anyone except You.' Since, apart from Him, no one exists in either world, Who, apart from Him, can be the object of love and desire? This is the meaning of prayer: 'God's Friend does not repent of infidelity, which is the opposite of faith.' [. . .] Infidelity is the abode of enmity, but faith is the abode of love" (p. 86).

"Fear of God is the gateway to bliss and the door to wealth. All the dwelling places that have been prepared in the world of 'There is no god but God' have been prepared for those who fear God, and all the abodes constructed in paradise are reserved for those who fear God. It should be known that anyone who fears God has been delivered from the miseries of self and has escaped the knot of self, for a man cannot be purified until he escapes from himself as well as from all traffic with his own self" (p. 258).

John Cassian: "Since you have asked me to repeat it, I will briefly explain the method of keeping our hearts still. Three things keep a wandering mind in place—vigils, meditation, and prayer. Constant attention to them and a firm concentration upon them will give stability to the soul. [. . .] This is the way to break out of the worries and the cares of the present life and to make possible for us the realization of the apostolic injunction 'Pray without cease' " (p. 139).

"All that was revealed to him at that stage occurred while he was at prayer. He heard God's word without any intermediary and was greatly enlightened by the disclosure of hidden things. Sparks shot forth for the fire of zeal burning in his heart" (p. 125).

Mind/imaging

Jacob Boehme: "Therefore his prayer is also to be so directed that it does not run against God's order. Rather, [he] is to think that in his prayer he will work with God as the wood on the tree works with the tree's power. So he is also to wish to work with God's power, or else his prayer will only be a shell of the true tree of life, for he works with it only externally in the elements and not internally and with God" (p. 78).

"Let him resolve and firmly commit his will to his resolution that he never again will wish to enter the old bestial images and evil, and even if all his pigs and beasts mourn for their herdsman" (p. 69).

Catherine of Siena: "Indeed, this soul remembered well what Truth had taught her: that she should always know herself and God's goodness at work in her, and that the medicine by which he willed to heal the whole world and to soothe his wrath and divine justice was humble, constant, holy prayer. So, spurred on by holy desire, she roused herself even more to open the eye of her understanding. She gazed into divine charity and there she saw and tasted how bound we are to love and seek the glory of God's name through the salvation of souls. She saw that God's servants are called to this—and in particular eternal Truth had called and chosen her spiritual father, whom she brought before the divine goodness, asking God to light within him a lamp of grace by which he might in truth pursue this Truth" (p. 57).

"Oh, how delightful to the soul and pleasing to me is holy prayer made in the house of self-knowledge and knowledge of me!" (p. 123).

"Thus you know of the glorious Thomas Aquinas that he gained his knowledge more from the study of prayer and the lifting up of his mind and the light of understanding than from human study!" (p. 181).

Abraham Isaac Kook: "Prayer and outcries to God and penitence from the depths of the heart expressed in a mending of behavior must precede every grasp of a higher perception. It is impossible for a truly important literature radiant with life-giving illumination to appear without the energizing presence of penitence, which renews the character of the whole world" (p. 78).

"Every prayer shall be illumined by the hidden light, the

universal light that is hidden in the higher soul before [its] efficacy begins to be manifested in action" (p. 206).

"In the light of all this, eating before prayer is very difficult, for it is difficult to gain the spiritual disposition needed to differentiate and select the good before enhancing one's spiritual state to evaluate life through prayer. Therefore all eating and drinking before prayer is in the category of pride" (p. 160).

"The inner enlightenment that wells up forcefully within the person, and the enlightenment from without, the rational, that derives from the knowledge of the world and of reality, both contribute to building the human spirit. They perfect one's understanding and will, and they function jointly, even when a person is not conscious of it" (p. 206).

Robert Bellarmine: "The fruits of prayer are principally three: merit, satisfaction, and receiving what we ask for. [. . .] Besides these three primary fruits there are many others. First, prayer enlightens the mind. For man cannot intently fix the eyes of the mind upon God who is light and not be enlightened by him. [. . .] Second, prayer nourishes faith and trust. For the more frequently one converses with another, the more confidently he approaches him. Third, prayer kindles love and prepares the mind to receive greater gifts, as Saint Augustine says. Fourth, prayer increases humility and holy fear. For one coming to prayer realizes that he is a beggar before God and, as a result, usually stands more humbly before him. And one who needs God's help in all things is most careful to avoid offending him. Fifth, frequent prayer leads to a contempt for all temporal things in the heart of the one who prays. For all earthly things inevitably become cheap and soiled for one who steadily gazes upon things heavenly and eternal" (pp. 262–63).

John Eudes: "The first [way of praying] is what we call mental or interior prayer, in which the soul converses interiorly with God, taking as a subject for this encounter one of his divine perfections or some mystery, virtue or word of the Son of God or what he has accomplished or now accomplishes in the order of glory, grace, nature or in his blessed Mother, in the saints, in his church or in the natural world. The soul begins by applying his understanding, with a gentle and firm attention and effort of the mind, to consider the truths contained in the chosen subject, and which are able to incite the soul to love God and detest his sins" (p. 315).

Abraham Isaac Kook: "And let him offer prayer to his Maker that he be enabled to realize in action those aspects of penitence that still remain unfulfilled, for his own sake, for the sake of all Israel and the whole world, and for the sake of the *shekhinah*, that the light of God shine in the world in all its fullness; and let him look forward to the time when all souls will be mended and enjoy the radiance of the divine presence, and all will be sated with goodness and with abounding life" (p. 66).

Thomas Aquinas: "It follows, then, that prayer is an act of the reason, bringing the will's desire into relationship with him who is our superior, not subject to our control, namely God" (p. 369).

"In response to the first question, we must say that three things are achieved by being specific in what we pray for: First, it helps us to focus our attention while we pray, and this is very necessary in prayer. Secondly, it makes us aware of our own desire and of how we are progressing in it. Thirdly, it makes us pray more fervently, because the more precisely we concentrate our attention on particular good things, the more earnestly we desire them, as the philosopher remarks in connection with bodily delights in the *Ethics*" (p. 397).

"Both mental and vocal prayer count as works of satisfaction, provided they are made in charity. [. . . Although mental prayer] is enjoyable, there is a certain painfulness attached to it too. As Gregory says, 'To pray is to utter bitter groans in a state of compunction,' either because of one's sins or because of one's delay in reaching heaven. Furthermore the raising of the mind is itself an affliction to the flesh [. . .] and any affliction of the flesh affects the mind too, inasmuch as they are united with one another, and it also affects the proud spirit, whose wound is healed by prayer. Prayer cannot be humble without a certain element of pain" (pp. 413–14).

Mind/emptying of images

Johannes Tauler: "[A spiritual-minded person] should recollect himself in the central point of his soul and raise his heart to God with great might, inwardly gazing upon God's presence, and ardently longing for whatever is dearest to God's will. He should die to self and to all created things and immerse himself ever deeper in God's most holy will" (p. 137).

"With the light of his reason [the inward regenerate person] swiftly surveys his exterior faculties and instructs them in their activity; but inwardly he is immersed and drawn into

God, joyfully adhering to Him. And in this state he remains unhindered by his activity" (p. 140).

Hamilton de Graw (*The Shakers*): "When the Divine teacher announced the importance of retiring into the closet and in silent devotion sending forth the prayer, he announced one of the grandest truths that was ever presented for human acceptance.

"In the movements of life upward it is from the silent, the powerful forces from which is evolved the strength that is lifting toward the higher. [. . .] The powers which to-day are the most potent factors in the advancement of life move so silently that those who are looking for a great sign in the heavens which is to usher in a new and improved order of life, feel that nothing is being done because it is not heralded with the blast of trumpets and immediate destruction of all opposing elements.

" 'The kingdom of heaven is within.' From the internal to the external is the true order of development" (pp. 120–21).

Jacob Boehme: "The student said: 'How can I hear when I remain silent in thinking and willing?' The master said: 'When you remain silent from the thinking and willing of self, the eternal hearing, seeing and speaking will be revealed in you, and God will see and hear through you. Your own hearing, willing and seeing hinders you so that you do not see and hear God' " (p. 171).

Meister Eckhart: "The most powerful prayer, and almost the strongest of all to obtain everything, and the most honorable of all works, is that which proceeds from an empty spirit. The emptier the spirit, the more is the prayer and the work mighty, worthy, profitable, praiseworthy and perfect. The empty spirit can do everything. What is an empty spirit? An empty spirit is one that is confused by nothing, attached to nothing, has not attached its best to any fixed way of acting, and has no concern whatever in anything for its own gain, for it is all sunk down into God's dearest will and has forsaken its own" (p. 248: *The Essential Sermons*).

Gregory Palamas: "It is of this [union of the mind with God] that the Fathers speak when they say, 'The end of prayer is to be snatched away to God.' This is why the great Denys says that through prayer, we are united to God. For in prayer, the mind gradually abandons all relation with created things: first with all things evil and bad, then with neutral things capable of conformity to either good or ill, according to the intentions of the person using them. It is to this last category that all studies belong and the knowledge that comes through them. Hence the Fathers warn us against accepting the knowledge that comes from the Enemy at the time of prayer, so as not to be deprived of that which is superior.

"Thus the mind slowly abandons all relation with these things, and even with those superior to them, in order to be totally separated from all beings through pure prayer. [. . .] But it is not yet union, unless the Paraclete illumines from on high the man who attains in prayer the stage which is superior to the highest natural possibilities, and who is awaiting the promise of the Father; and by His revelation ravishes him to the contemplation of the light. [. . .] But is the union with this light other than a vision? And since it is brought about by the cessation of intellectual activity, how could it be accomplished if not by the Spirit?" (p. 65).

Johannes Tauler: "Just as my cloak and my clothes are not me and yet serve me, so also vocal prayer serves and leads occasionally to true prayer, although it falls short of being that by itself. For true prayer is a direct raising of the mind and heart to God, without intermediary. This and nothing else is the essence of prayer" (p. 89).

Maximus Confessor: "It is said that the supreme state of prayer is when the mind passes outside the flesh and the world and while praying is completely without matter and form. The one who preserves this state without compromise really 'prays without ceasing' " (p. 55).

Nicodemos of the Holy Mountain: "Let your inner understanding say only the Jesus Prayer; let your mind pay attention through its spiritual vision and hearing to the words of the prayer only and especially to the meaning of the words, without any forms or shapes and without imagining any other perceptible or intelligible thing internal or external, even if it is good. Because God transcends all beings both visible and invisible, the human mind seeking to be united with him through prayer must go out of all beings that are perceptible or intelligible in order to achieve this divine union. There, as St. Neilos said: 'While you are praying do not attempt to give shape to the divine, nor allow any image to be impressed upon your mind, but approach the spiritual spiritually and you shall understand' " (p. 159).

◊

It may be helpful to work through these same quotations from the perspective of one's most recent or most characteristic experience of worship and church services. How we pray is shaped in part by our experiences of worship together; it is well to name the type of approach to prayer which is presumed in our public worship.

5. Sin and Forgiveness

*T*his question asks simply, "What is sin?" Sin is an important reality in the awareness of all who seek God. Sin, like grace, is always part and parcel of the devout life. The more we know God's grace, the more we are aware of our distance from the One who is Gracious; the more we know God's compassion, the more we are aware of our lack of compassion for our brothers and sisters and all the earth.

As you begin to answer this question for yourself, keep in mind that sin is a *religious* word—that is, it is a word which only makes sense when we know ourselves to be in relation to God. Sin is part of a world which speaks as well of forgiveness, of grace, of conversion, of hardness of heart. Outside of this religious context we may speak of moral fault, ethical failure, vice, failing, and so on. These words are not directly part of a religious understanding of the world. Keep in mind, too, that sin and guilt are not the same realities: sin refers to a relationship with God, guilt refers to a relationship with ourself. Guilt is a set of self-punishing feelings which serves (ideally) to protect us from repeating an unwanted or undesirable act.

"Sin" is a religious word! We might almost say that sin is a religious activity—although that might be pushing the case too far. As strange as it may seem, sin and the horror of sin are really understood only when seen within the context of God's compassion. An example might make this clearer. We

70

would feel deeply—too deeply for words—the tragic death of our best friend in an accident caused by drunken driving. But only we who know and love this person could experience the full tragedy of the event. Drunken driving is one thing; drunken driving that kills our best friend reveals its true horror. In the same way, it takes *love* (God's love) to know what sin really is. In knowing it, we also know—indeed we come to focus on—God.

As you trace your life's journey and explore the light and shadows of your spiritual life, let your awareness of your sin and sins become real and intense; but never let it degenerate into self-loathing—an ugly deviation from attention to God. The readings which follow may, indeed, surprise and comfort you.

When you have reflected and written your reflections, we invite you to turn to the texts, beginning with the approach with which you are most comfortable.

Heart/imaging

Symeon the New Theologian: "Before all else, pray to be given tears, that weeping may soften the savage hardness which is in your soul and, having acknowledged your sin unto the Lord (Ps 31:5), you may receive from Him the remission of sins" (p. 31).

"When he has been left alone he sees himself in the midst of solitude, misery, affliction, and pain. So he will weep in the pain of his soul, and in his despair cry out to the Lord Almighty: 'Behold, O Lord, Thou seest, and there is nothing Thou dost not see. I am the work of Thy hands, yet I have not performed the works of Thy commandments, but in my folly I have followed after all wickedness. Thou art good, yet I did not know Thee, but now I have heard of Thee and I tremble and do not know what to do. I have perceived Thy judgment, and no word in my defense was found in my mouth' [. . .].

"So God in His compassion will speedily hear him and will hasten to grant him relief from his pain and deliverance from the distress of his heart. For since he loves man He cannot bear to see the work of His hands in such need and in such intolerable pain" (pp. 255–56).

Julian of Norwich: "We shall be rewarded in heaven by the courteous love of our almighty God, who does not wish anyone who comes there to lose his labors in any degree. For he regards sin as sorrow and pain for his lovers, to whom for love he assigns no blame" (p. 245).

"Man is changeable in this life, and falls into sin through naiveté and ignorance. He is weak and foolish in himself, and also his will is overpowered in the time when he is assailed and in sorrow and woe. And the cause is blindness, because he does not see God, for if he saw God continually, he would have no harmful feelings nor any kind of prompting, no sorrowing which is conducive to sin" (p. 260).

"He is here alone with us all; that is to say, he is here only for us. And when I am distant towards him through sin, despair or sloth, then I leave my Lord to remain alone, inasmuch as he is in me. And this is the case with us all who are sinners; but though it may be that we act like this often, his goodness never allows us to be alone, but constantly he is with us, and tenderly he excuses us, and always protects us from blame in his sight" (p. 336).

Francis of Assisi: "And by this I wish to know if you love the Lord God and me, his servant and yours [. . .]—that is, there should not be any brother in the world who has sinned, however much he may have possibly sinned, who, after he has looked into your eyes, would go away without having received your mercy, if he is looking for mercy" (p. 75).

"And let all the brothers, both the ministers and servants as well as the others, take care not to be disturbed or angered at the sin or the evil of another, because the devil wishes to destroy many through the fault of one; but they should spiritually help the brother who has sinned as best they can, because it is not the healthy who are in need of the physician, but those who are sick" (p. 113).

Julian of Norwich: "No more than his love towards us is withdrawn because of our sin does he wish our love to be withdrawn from ourselves or from our fellow Christians" (p. 243).

"For our courteous Lord does not want his servants to despair because they fall often and grievously; for our falling does not hinder him in loving us" (p. 245).

Bernard of Clairvaux: "And after he finds that his first sins go unpunished by the terrible judgment of God (Heb 10:27), he freely seeks to enjoy again the pleasures he has experienced. Habit binds him as desire revives, and conscience slumbers. The wretched man is dragged into the depths of evil (Prv 18:3) and handed over captive to the tyranny of the vices as though to be swallowed up in the whirlpool of fleshly desires; and he forgets the fear of God and his own reason. The fool says in his heart, 'There is no God' (Ps 13:1)" (p. 138).

"The third task remains and that is the hardest: to purify the memory. [. . .] Take a thin piece of poor-quality parchment which has soaked up the ink with which the scribe has written on it. Can any skill erase it? [. . .] It would be pointless for me to try to clean it. The parchment would tear before the marks of wretchedness were removed. Forgetting would perhaps destroy the memory itself, so that, in a mental convulsion, I should cease to remember what I had done. We must ask, then, what keen edge can both clean my memory and keep it intact? Only the living and effective Word which is sharper than a two-edge sword (Heb 4:12) which 'takes away your sins' (Mk 2:5)" (pp. 87–88).

Catherine of Genoa: "God also showed the creature how patiently His love waited, how He abhorred many sins; for had the soul died then and there it would have been perpetually damned. Her soul, he showed her, had come close to death. He alone in the gentlest of ways had saved her, acting on her with such tender affection that she was virtually forced to do His will. [. . .] That merciful love, Catherine saw, penetrates as deep as hell (pp. 108–9).

Francisco de Osuna: "To return to the two things that should grieve you, the first is sadness over sin, which usually arises from our displeasure at offending God. If this sadness is true contrition infused and caused by God in the soul, the sorrow is so intense that it seems to shatter the heart, bursting forth and causing most bitter tears [. . .]" (p. 376).

Heart/emptying of images

John Woolman: "But in this swift race it pleased God to visit me with sickness, so that I doubted of recovering. And then did darkness, horror, and amazement with full force seize me, even when my pain and distress of body was very great. I thought it would have been better for me never to have had a being than to see the day which I now saw. I was filled with confusion, and in great affliction both of mind and body I lay and bewailed myself. I had not confidence to lift up my cries to God, whom I had thus offended, but in a deep sense of my great folly I was humbled before him, and at length that word which is as a fire and a hammer broke and dissolved my rebellious spirit. And then my cries were put up in contrition, and in the multitude of his mercies I found inward relief, and felt a close engagement that if he was pleased to restore my health, I might walk humbly before him" (pp. 164–65).

Isaac Pennington: "It is your proper state to wait daily, not for comforts, not for refreshments (that day is to come afterwards), but for convictions and proofs of that in you which is contrary to God. . . . You must die to your own wisdom if ever ye will be born of a walk in the wisdom of God" (p. 146).

The Pursuit of Wisdom: "So come down to the lowest point of your understanding, which some maintain by experience to be the highest, and think in the most ignorant way, which some maintain to be the wisest, not what your own self is, but *that* it is. Because to think what you are according to your distinctive qualities requires great learning and intellectual ability, and very skillful investigation into your natural faculties. You have been doing this now for some time, with the help of grace, so that you now have some knowledge—as much, I suppose, as is good for you at the moment —that you are a man by nature, and by sin a foul stinking wretch. You know well how it is; and sometimes it seems to you that you know too well the various filths that pursue and attach to wretched man. Fie on them! Leave them alone, I pray you" (pp. 221–22).

"When by the grace of God and after long striving a man comes to the experience of spiritual joy in God, then he appreciates that sin has been the cause of this delay. And when he also appreciates that he cannot continue to experience that spiritual joy because of the corruptible nature of the flesh, of which sin is the cause, then there arises in him a strong hatred of all sin and of every sinful quality" (p. 30).

✓   **John Ruusbroec:** "The grace of God is the path we must always follow if we are to arrive at that bare being in which God gives himself to us without intermediary in all his richness. Sinners and the damned spirits are in darkness precisely because they lack God's grace, which would have enlightened them, instructed them, and led them to this blissful unity. Nevertheless the essential being of the spirit is so noble that the damned cannot will their own annihilation [. . .]. Whoever lives apart from sin lives in the likeness and grace of God and has God as his own possession" (p. 120).

"When a person has done all that he can and is able to proceed no further because of his own weakness, then it falls to the fathomless goodness of God to bring the work to completion. Thus there arises a higher light of God's grace which, like a ray of sunlight, is cast upon the soul without its being merited or desired in a way commensurate with its worth. [. . .] From this grace of God and this free conversion of a will that has been enlightened by grace, charity is born, that is, divine love, and from divine love there arises the third thing that is required if a person is to see in a supernatural way, namely, a purification of his conscience. [. . .] Whoever has divine love necessarily has perfect sorrow for his sins" (pp. 45–46).

✓ **Henry Suso:** "A root of all sin and a clouding of all truth is transitory love" (p. 182).

Hadewijch: "There are two ways in which persons may help others. The first way consists in extending a hand to sinners in their overthrow. A man is sometimes so wounded by charity for others that he must renounce the fruition and blessedness of God for the sake of sinners who live in sin, preferring to be deprived of his Beloved until assurance is given him that these sinners are not despairing of God's grace (Rom 9:3)" (p. 51).

The Cloud of Unknowing: "If, then, you are determined to stand and not to fall, never cease from your endeavour, but constantly beat with a sharp dart of longing love upon this cloud of unknowing which is between you and your God. Avoid thinking of anything under God and do not leave this exercise no matter what happens. For it alone, of itself, destroys the root and the ground of sin" (p. 145).

Angelus Silesius:
The praise that God the Lord from unjust one receives
Is much less loved by Him than a dog's barking is
    (p. 113).

Mind/imaging

Pseudo-Dionysius: "As for your inhumanity toward this man whom you declare to be impious and sinful, I do now know how I am going to bewail the ruin of someone dear to me. [. . .] Have we ourselves been so perfected to complete holiness that we do not need that love for humanity which God has shown to us? As scripture says, do we not sin like impious men in a double sin first by not knowing how we offend and, secondly, by justifying ourselves on our own account and by thinking we see what in fact we do not see? Heaven was appalled at this, and I was shocked at it myself and could hardly believe it" (p. 276).

Jacob Boehme: "When a man wishes to proceed to repentance, and turn himself to God with his prayers, he is to examine his mind before any prayer, considering how it is completely and wholly turned from God; how it has become faithless to God; how it is ordered only in the temporal, fragile, earthly life and directs no correct love to God or its neighbor; and how it thus lusts and seethes against God's law and seeks only itself in temporal, perishable, fleshly lust" (pp. 27–28).

"Saint Paul does not intend that the mind is to will with the flesh's will, but that sin is as strong in the flesh as the aroused wrath of God is in the self, that it is, often by force or by false approval of godless men or by means of a glimpse of worldly pomp, led into a lust so that the resigned will is completely deafened and is soon ruled by force" (pp. 128–29).

John Eudes: "Now we must continue in ourselves those same sentiments that Jesus had toward his Father and toward sin. [. . .] To motivate yourselves for this, from now on look at sin not as men see it, with carnal and blind eyes, but as God sees it, with eyes enlightened by his divine light, that is, with eyes of faith. With this light and these eyes, you will see sin as in some way infinitely contrary and opposed to God and all his divine perfections and as a deprivation of an infinite good, which is God. Thus it contains in itself a malice, a foolishness, an ugliness and a horror as great, in a sense, as God's infinite goodness, wisdom, beauty and holiness. Therefore, sin should be hated and persecuted as much as God deserves to be sought after and loved" (p. 301).

Catherine of Siena: "This is the endowment I gave to all of you, and I your Father expect a return from it. But if you sell it in barter to the devil, the devil goes off with it and carries away everything you had acquired in this life. Then he fills your memory with delightful recollections of indecency, pride, avarice, selfish love for yourself, and hatred and contempt for your neighbors. (For the devil is a persecutor of my servants.) Your mind is darkened in these wretched things by your disordered will, and so in stench you reap eternal punishment, infinite punishment, for you would not atone for your guilt with contrition and contempt for sin.

"So you see, suffering atones for sin not by reason of the finite pain but by reason of perfect contrition of the heart. And in those who have this perfect contrition it atones not only for the sin itself but for the penalty due that sin" (p. 32).

Abraham Isaac Kook: "The basic disposition to penitence is inspired by the sense of the awesome perfection of the divine, and it is this that causes sin to be glaringly conspicuous. 'You have placed our iniquities before You, our secret sins in the light of Your presence' (Ps. 90:8). The very realization that the feeling of being in a state of sin comes, in every case, as a result of a divine illumination acting on the soul—this very thought engenders endless joy and exultation" (p. 116).

"As long as man has not repented of his sin, has not yet arranged his order of penitence, he remains under the servitude of his own choice and his guilt for all his misdeeds, and all their evil consequences weigh on him. However, after the process of penitence has begun, all his life's deficiencies, all his misdeeds and their bitter results, are transferred into the divine domain and all are reassessed outside the factor of his own freedom and his choice; they are merged within the domain of the higher providence, the providence of God, who effectuated all our works" (p. 120).

Humbert of Romans: "Notice that there are three factors which make it difficult for people to abandon their sins. The first is sensual pleasure, which is the devil's birdlime. This is why it is difficult to abandon the sin of fornication, because there is particularly intense sensual pleasure in this sin. [. . .] The second is habit, because, as Augustine says, 'A habit which is not resisted becomes a need.' [. . .] The third is notoriety. Once his sin has become notorious, a man acquires the 'cheek of a harlot' and loses all sense of shame, and so comes to be all the more hardened in his sin. The Gloss on Matt. 18:15, 'Take him aside and rebuke him between yourselves' says that this is to avoid making him lose all shame and so remain in his sin" (p. 361).

Mind/emptying of images

One brief note: The first text, that of Tauler, gives an insight into why he chose techniques of emptying of images; namely, he was aware of the inroads of disordered self-love even when one thinks one has found God.

✓   **Johannes Tauler:** "Not that God made our nature like this; it has become corrupted and disfigured by turning away from Him. So deeply rooted is this poison in the inmost recesses of the soul that all the experts in the world cannot trace all its ramifications, nor will they ever succeed in rooting it out. This corrupt tendency very often comes to light when one thinks one has found God. [. . .] Corrupt nature constantly makes its inroads, and before we are aware of it everything is flooded with disordered self-love" (p. 82).

William Law: "For all sins, whether of sensuality, pride, or falseness, or any other irregular passion, are nothing else but the filthy and impure diseases of the rational soul. And all righteousness is nothing else but the purity, the decency, the beauty and perfection of that spirit which is made in the image of God" (p. 335).

✓ **Meister Eckhart:** "The heavier a man's sins are as he weighs them, the readier is God to forgive them, and to come to the soul, and to drive the sins out. Every man does his utmost to get rid of what most irks him. And the greater and the more the sins are, still immeasurably more is God glad and ready to forgive them, because they are irksome to him. And then, as godly repentance lifts itself up to God, sins vanish into God's abyss, faster than it takes me to shut my eyes, and so they become utterly nothing, as if they had never happened, if repentance is complete" (p. 263).

✓ **Origen:** "Everyone who sins hides himself from God, flees His coming, and is removed from boldness" (p. 128).

"I believe that the words of the saints' prayers are filled with power, especially when praying with the Spirit they also pray with the mind (cf. 1 Cor 14:15). Then the mind is like light rising from the understanding of the one who prays [. . .]. For it goes forth from the soul of the one praying like an arrow shot from the saint by knowledge and reason and faith. And it wounds the spirits hostile to God to destroy and overthrow them when they wish to hurl round us the bonds of sin" (p. 104).

Maximus Confessor: "Humility and distress free man from every sin, the former by cutting out the passions of the soul, the latter those of the body" (p. 43).

"As much as it is easier to sin in thought than in deed, so is a war with thoughts more exacting than one with things" (p. 57).

Martin Luther: "All concerns about the I, Mine, self, and things connected with them must be utterly lost and surrendered, except, of course, the traits that are necessary for our existence as persons. Thereby we tune into God whose innermost characteristic is such freedom. What happens in a truly divinized person, be it in action or silent suffering compassion, happens in this Light and in this Love. [. . .] That person does not complain about anything but the power of sin. What sin is, we have previously called the desire to seek something other than the simple, perfect Truth and the one eternal Will. To put it differently: to assert self-will in independence of and against eternal Will" (p. 127).

6. Presence of God

 T he fifth set of questions inquires in a variety of ways about the presence of God: "Where is the presence of God to be found?" "How do you know?" "What is the presence of God like?" "What, if any, images of God are helpful to you?" These questions relate to the experience of the presence (or absence) of God. They invite us to try to name our experience. Perhaps more so than with some aspects of the spiritual life previously mentioned, the experience of the presence of God varies over the years. It is important to try to remember how God's presence made itself known to us at the various ages of our life in order to appreciate our own journeys and to be open to the variety of experiences of the Presence to which the following texts are witness. Thus we invite you to take time to get hold of this rich part of your spiritual life. Perhaps it will be helpful to go decade by decade, and to single out major events in your outer and inner lives. Again we refer you to Appendix C. There you will find suggestions for getting in touch with the important events of your outer life (school, graduation, work, births and deaths, etc.). You will also find suggestions for getting in touch with your inner life (memories, insights, growth, self-transcendence, etc.). Again, we invite you to take time for this exploration. Your questions, your reality, your experiences are the places of God's self-showing. When we speak of the presence of God, we are looking squarely at your life, your experience, and your world.

We have asked how you know that a "presence" is the Presence of God. The question implies that there can be false presences and that every presence is incomplete. No doubt the passing of the years has brought us the experience of what has been called the "dark night of the senses" or the "dark night of the soul," and we have perhaps come to mistrust some of our earlier experiences. There is no need to deny in the darkness what we have known in the light. Some very incomplete presences, full of what we may now see to be childish consolation and satisfaction, have sustained us at those times when we could bear no presence more adequate to the Divine Mystery. It is simply important to remember, to note, to give thanks.

The present experience of the Presence will have a particular sense of urgency to it. It is in the here and now that you will engage the texts we offer. They are rich and powerful, as they relate directly to the experience of others of God's friends. When you have written your response, please move on to the texts. You may wish to come back and add to your own answers as the words of others spark memories and insights.

Heart/imaging

Luis de León: "God's union with our soul takes place all of a sudden, without the foreplay that is so typical of our bodily union between man and woman. It is more intense and more lasting than our human sexual union, more stable and all embracing, and this is why the Psalms state that there is a river flowing with God's grace, not drop by drop, but as a strong current.

"In conclusion, the marriage of God and our soul is a source of pleasure, delight, and bliss, that nothing can surpass. It is never mixed with doubt or anguish or sadness, it is never tarnished, there is nothing rough or superficial about it. It is an abundant source of joy, it bathes our soul in joy, it makes us drunk with bliss.

"Therefore the Holy Scripture makes use of several images and metaphors when it tries to describe such a unique experience. It calls it sometimes 'hidden manna,' a special and sweet food—hidden because no one knows what takes place in our soul when God embraces us. It can also be described as a wine, or as a liquor better than wine, or as a cellar full of wine casks and bottles. It can be compared to breasts full of milk to be enjoyed by a baby, for God's presence is even sweeter and more comforting than the mother's breast offering milk to her baby. It is also said that God finds a dwelling place in the middle or center of our heart" (pp. 251–52).

Julian of Norwich: "A creature should see the Lord marvelously great, and herself marvelously little. For these virtues are endlessly brought to God's beloved, and when this happens, it can now to some extent be seen and felt through our Lord's gracious presence. In every circumstance this presence is most desired, for it creates that wonderful security in true faith and certain hope, by a greatness of love in fear which is sweet and delectable" (p. 308).

"Our Lord showed me a spiritual sight of his familiar love. I saw that he is to us everything which is good and comforting for our help. He is our clothing, for he is that love which wraps and enfolds us, embraces us and guides us, surrounds us for his love, which is so tender that he may never desert us. And so in this sight I saw truly that he is everything which is good, as I understand" (p. 130).

Francisco de Osuna: " 'Walk in the ways of your heart.'

Like man-made roads, the ways of the heart crumble from disuse, but if used, they become wider and clearer. And so if you destroy the ways of your heart through neglect, it is no wonder you do not know how to journey on them. Return to them, return, and may the person and spirit you are always go as one. Do not be like Cain, who left the presence of God and wandered like a fugitive and vagabond over the earth" (p. 54).

"The evil fear the presence which the good love" (p. 303).

Johann Arndt: "How glorious, precious, and lovely is it that our highest and best treasure, the kingdom of God, is not an external but an internal good that we continually carry with us, hidden from all the world and the Devil himself, which neither the world nor the Devil can take from us. For it, we need no great knowledge of languages, learning, or many books, but a resigned heart given to God. [. . .] What can we seek externally in the world if we have internally in ourselves everything and the whole kingdom of God with all his goods? In our hearts and souls is the true school of the Holy Spirit, the true working place of the Holy Trinity, the true temple of God (1 Cor 6:19), the true house of prayer, in spirit and in truth (Jn 4:24). Although God, by his general presence, is in all things, and not bound up in them, but in an inconceivable way fills heaven and earth, in a special and characteristic way his is in the enlightened soul of man in which he lives and has his seat (Is 66:1,2). There, in his own image and likeness, he enacts those works that he himself is. There in the heart he continually answers our sighs. How is it possible for him to deny them in persons in whom he has his dwelling; indeed, how is it possible for him to deny those concerns that he himself moves and bears? Nothing is more lovely and pleasant for him than to give himself to those who seek him.

 "For this to come about, a refined, silent, and peaceful soul is necessary. The soul will be peaceful and still if it turns from the world" (pp. 222–23).

Francisco de Osuna: "The entire world, therefore, cannot fill the tiny heart of man [. . .]. The reason for this is that the world is empty of genuine goodness and so cannot supply the heart with what it does not possess. Thus the heart must be filled either with joy in the Lord's presence or sadness that he has departed so as not to appear empty before the One who is as much pleased by the soul's sadness as its happiness and who, as promised, turns the sadness into joy. It may even be that sadness caused by his absence pleases the Lord even more than happiness, for our grief at lack of something reveals our great love for it. If we were quickly consoled for a loss, that would be a sign that our love was slight, but intense sadness is evidence of intense love" (p. 380).

Heart/emptying of images

The first text of this section is by Francisco de Osuna— as was the last text of the previous section. We vacillated about the placing of the previous text but in the end decided that the phrase "intense sadness is evidence of intense love" warranted its inclusion in the heart/*imaging* approach. In contrast, the text which follows, with its appeal to silence of imagination, memory, and our very selves, seemed to fit better in the heart/*emptying of images* approach. We leave it to the reader to discover what chord these texts strike and how the reader may best enter into conversation with our brother, Francisco de Osuna.

Nor is it clear that the first Fakhruddin ʿIraqi text belongs in this section. We have chosen to place it here, in spite of its image richness, because of the last line which seems to indicate the futility of any image of God.

Francisco de Osuna: "It is proper to be very quiet and attentive to God. Thus there are two kinds of silence: In the one the imagination and thought revolving in memory are calm; in the other we become forgetful of our very selves, and the interior person is in perfect communion with God alone.

"The first silence is with respect to other things as they concern us; the second is a deep rest wherein we become quiet to ourselves and turn to God with expectant, open submissiveness" (p. 560).

Fakhruddin ʿIraqi: The shadow-play master behind the screen performs his contradictory mummery, his diverse turns and steps, jugglery and props, all him, and hid behind the scrim. When they strike the set you'll know these shapes and their posturings for what they really are:

the whole show but one
    lone puppeteer
hid behind his
    screen of art.
He tears it away
    reveals himself alone
and all illusions
    vanish into nothing. (Ibn al-Farid)

His presence is a sun
    and heaven and earth

I find are but
  a parasol . . . (p. 103).

The lover's duty: to like what the Friend approves, even
if it be nothing but remoteness and separation. And in fact,
this is usually the case, for He wants us to seek refuge from
His cruelty in Love; "Hellfire is a whip to drive God's people
to God" (H) perhaps alludes to something of this sort. The
lover must like his own exile and submit to separation, finding his habit in this line:

I want Union with Him
  He wants separation for me—
so I abandon my desire
  to His.

He likes separation not in itself but only because the Beloved
likes it.

All the Beloved does
  is lovable.

So what can the poor lover do? What can he say except,

"Searching for separation
  yearning for Union
I am free of both:
  Thy love suffices."

Hadewijch:
Although daylight and the season are drear,
May God be blessed for everything!
  We shall soon behold better.
Love, your being so far from me—

> Whereas all my delight must come from you—
> Remains a constant grief.
>   But that is self-evident:
>   All that gives light to my heart,
>   By which I should live,
>   Searches for you in your totality.
>   See what must befall me:
>   Nothing whatever is left to me!
>
> Alas, how should anything content me, Love,
>   save you in your totality?
> It is my lot that I do not possess you fully,
>   And that I cannot fully content you with
> Veritable, high-minded, and lavish love.
> Were anyone to give you anything less,
> That would be a great insult to you.
>   For you ask total love,
>   *With heart and with mind*
> *And with the whole soul* (pp. 199–200).

The Zohar: "Happy are Israel! They are privileged to hold this pledge of the Supreme King! For even though they are in exile, every new moon and Sabbath and festival the Blessed Holy One comes to watch over them and to gaze at His pledge which is with them, His treasure. A parable: There was a king whose queen offended him. He expelled her from the palace. What did she do? She took his son, his precious beloved. Since the king was fond of her, he let him go with her. When the king began to yearn for the queen and her son he climbed up on roofs, ran down stairs, scaled walls; he peered through holes in the walls just to see them! When he caught a glimpse of them he started to cry from behind the wall. Then he went away" (pp. 156–57).

"So, the Blessed Holy One desired to dwell with Israel.

What did He do? He took his most precious possession and brought it down to them, saying 'Israel, now you have My pledge; so I will never part from you.'

"Even though the Blessed Holy One has removed Himself from us, He has left a pledge in our hands, and we guard that treasure of His. If He wants His pledge, let Him come and dwell among us!" (p. 154).

"Come and see the pure love of the Blessed Holy One for Israel. A parable: There was a king who had a single son who kept misbehaving. One day he offended the king. The king said, 'I have punished you so many times and you have not received. Now look, what should I do with you? If I banish you from the land and expel you from the kingdom, perhaps wild beasts or wolves will attack you and you will be no more. What can I do? The only solution is that I and you together leave the land. . .' " (pp. 159–60).

George Herbert:
Whither, Oh, whither art thou fled,
    My Lord, my Love?
My searches are my daily bread;
    Yet never prove.

My knees pierce th' earth, mine eyes the sky;
    And yet the sphere
And center both to me deny
    That thou art there.
. . . .
Where is my God? what hidden place
    Conceals thee still?
What covert dare eclipse they face?
    Is it thy will?
. . . .

When thou dost turn, and wilt be near;
    What edge so keen,
What point so piercing can appear
    To come between?

For as thy absence doth excel
    All distance known:
So doth thy nearness bear the bell,
    Making two one (pp. 286–88).

Jacapone da Todi:
Love beyond all telling,
Goodness beyond imagining,
Light of infinite intensity
Glows in my heart.

I once thought that reason
Had led me to You,
And that through feeling
I sensed Your presence,
Caught a glimpse of You in similitudes,
Knew You in Your perfection.
I know now that I was wrong,
That that truth was flawed.

Light beyond metaphor,
Why did You deign to come into this darkness?
Your light does not illumine those who think they see
    You
And believe they sound Your depths.
Night, I know now, is day,
Virtue no more to be found.
He who witnesses Your splendor
Can never describe it.

On achieving their desired end
Human powers cease to function,
And the soul sees that what it thought was right
Was wrong. A new exchange occurs
At that point where all light disappears;
A new and unsought state is needed:
The soul has what it did not love,
And is stripped of all it possessed, no matter how dear.

In God the spiritual faculties
Come to their desired end,
Lose all sense of self and self-consciousness,
And are swept into infinity.
The soul, made new again,
Marveling to find itself
In that immensity, drowns.
How this comes about it does not know.

It is within and sees no exit;
It no longer knows how to think of itself
Or to speak of the wondrous change.
It knows only that it finds itself
Clothed in new garments.
Fused with God, it ventures forth
Onto a sea without a shore
And gazes on Beauty without color or hue.

It hears
What it did not hear, sees what it did not know,
Possesses what it did not believe,
Savors that which has no taste.

Again **Jacopone da Todi:**

Faith and hope have estranged me from myself,
Struck at my heart, annihilated me.

Within and without I am shattered,
Reduced to nothingness:
This the fruit of centering my life on love.
I am no longer able to flee or to pursue;
Caught in the swell of the sea
I drown, and my words drown with me!

My speech is silence and shout.
I know where He is hidden, for though I see Him not
I recognize the signs of His presence
In every creature that is one with Him.
Being and nonbeing I have fused together,
And out of love banished my will with its "yes" and
    "no" (pp. 274–75).

Mind/imaging

Jacob Boehme: "O God, Fountain-source of love and
mercy, I praise and glorify You in Your truth, and thank You
in my heart that You offer to me Your face once more and
look on me, unworthy and wretched as I am, with the eyes of
Your mercy, and give me again a beam of comfort so that my
soul can hope on You. [. . .] The dry places of the heart and
soul you water with Your rain, and give them the water of
Your mercy. In the midst of death, You make them alive, and
set them before You so that they live. You make them think
of the mercy and covenant that you have made with us
through Your blood and death, and You forgive us our sins.
You give us your power that we may know You. [. . .] Now
does my soul know this; therefore it praises You and rejoices
in Your great might and majesty" (pp. 84–85).

Philo of Alexandria: "To souls that are still in a body he gives himself the appearance of angels, not altering his own nature for he is unchangeable, but implanting in those who form an impression of him a semblance of another form so that they take the image to be not a copy but that original form itself" (p. 221).

Robert Bellarmine: "This is a true mirror of God's existence in created things. God is an indivisible spirit; he nonetheless fills the whole world and all its parts without occupying any place. Rather he is whole in the whole world and whole in every part of the world. And when a new creature is produced, God begins to be in it, though he does not move. When a creature for some reason is destroyed or dies, God is not destroyed and does not die, but he ceases to be there though without changing his position. [. . .] God is in absolutely everything, not only in bodily things but also spiritual beings; nothing can come into existence without God being in it. [. . .] Hence, if other heavens and another earth came to be, he would also be in them; and further if new heavens and new earths were multiplied endlessly, he would fill them all, and where he was not, there would be nothing at all" (p. 139).

Menahem Nahum of Chernobyl: "Torah [the first of the three Jewish divisions of the Old Testament] is the spice that seasons and sweetens the evil urge. It is by means of the Torah that God causes His *shekhinah* [the presence of God on earth or its manifestation] to dwell within a human being. Thus Scripture says: 'Let them make Me a sanctuary that I may dwell within them' (Ex 25:8). It is known that the light of the Infinite, blessed be He, shines forth and dwells in the letters of Torah. When a person attaches his inner life-force and his words to the Torah, that life within Him is bound to the portion of divinity that shines forth from Torah's letters. Such is the case of one who studies with this intent, and has no ulterior motivations or extraneous goals. This person is himself also called a 'sanctuary,' for by means of the longing and joy that reach Him from such service, God contracts His *shekhinah* so that it may enter that man" (p. 73).

"We have to understand Rabbi Eleazar's point here, that the lesser does not ask the greater to wait, and yet Abraham did so. Could we not say that there too, in the greeting of guests, there was a receiving of the *shekhinah?* This is especially so since the righteous are called 'the face of the *shekhinah*' in the Zohar, as His presence dwells in them. When Abraham received the guests, that is, the angels who appeared to him in human form, surely that in itself was an act of greeting the *shekhinah*" (p. 136).

John Eudes: "The third way of praying is to accomplish all your actions in a Christian and holy manner, even the least significant, offering them to our Lord when you begin them and lifting your heart to him from time to time where you are performing them [. . .]. For in this way, we perform our actions in a spirit of prayer. We are always in a continual exercise of prayer, faithful to our Lord's command that *we pray always and without interruption* (Lk 18:1, 1 Thes 5:17). It is a very excellent and quite easy way to remain always in the presence of God" (p. 316).

Abraham Isaac Kook: "At times the heart suffers inner distress without reason or cause. This emanates from the source of penitence. The lofty light of God's presence reveals itself in the depths of the soul in a highly circumscribed form. This seed needs considerable watering from the fountain of higher knowledge and then it will emerge into the world with many great and celebrated lights, illuminating the whole mystery of life. The tree of life, with its precious fruit, will then manifest itself to the soul, and the person will be elevated and hallowed, and his mourning will be turned to joy, and he will be consoled and gladdened out of his sorrow. 'Out of gloom and darkness, the eyes of the blind shall see' (Isa 29:18)" (p. 114).

"A person must liberate himself from confinement within his private concerns. This pervades his whole being so that all his thoughts focus only on his own destiny. It reduces him to the worst kind of smallness, and brings upon him endless physical and spiritual distress. It is necessary to raise a person's thought and will and his basic preoccupations toward universality, to the inclusion of all, to the whole world, to man, to the Jewish people, to all existence. This will result in establishing even his private self on a proper basis. The firmer a person's vision of universality, the greater the joy he will experience, and the more he will merit the grace of divine illumination. The reality of God's providence is discernible when the world is seen in its totality. God's presence is not manifest in anything defective. Since He does not abide where there is deficiency, how can He abide where anything is lacking, where all we have is the weak and puny entity, only the particularity of the ego?" (p. 232).

Teresa of Avila: "I tell you, Sisters, that the cross is not wanting but it doesn't disquiet or make them lose peace. For the storms, like a wave, pass quickly. And the fair weather returns, because the presence of the Lord they experience makes them soon forget everything. May he be ever blessed and praised by all His creatures, Amen" (pp. 187–88).

Maximus the Confessor: "The one who keeps untar-

nished the way of virtue with religious and upright knowledge and does not fall away will discover the presence of
God in him through detachment. 'I will sing and be wise in a
blameless path when you come to me.' The *psalm* means a
virtuous way of asceticism; *being wise* is the gnostic understanding which comes from virtue whereby one who waits
for the Lord in the watchfulness of the virtues experiences
the divine presence" (pp. 169–70).

Mind/emptying of images

The first of these texts is from a volume titled *Native
Mesoamerican Spirituality,* which includes ancient myths, discourses, stories, doctrines, hymns, poems from the Aztec,
Yucatec, Quiche-Maya and other sacred traditions. It may
evoke for some of our readers a presence of God within a
darkened spirit. The last of the quotes, that of Johannes
Tauler, approaches the "darkened spirit" in another way.
The soul, he says is "God-hued," and if we could but see the
soul we would see God. The implication is, however, that we
cannot see with our minds even the human soul, let
alone God.

The *Popol Vuh:* **The Book of Counsel:** "[The first men
who were made] spoke and talked; they saw and they heard;
they walked; they grasped [. . .]. They came to see; they came
to know everything under heaven if they could see it. [. . .]
Their understanding became great. Their gaze passed over
trees, rocks, lakes, seas, mountains, and valleys. Truly, then,
they were the most beloved of men, Jaguar Quiche, Jaguar
Night, Nought, and Wind Jaguar.

"And then they were asked by the Former and Shaper:
'How pleasant is your existence? Do you know? Can't you
see? Can't you hear? Isn't your language good and your

walking? And look now at what you see under heaven! Aren't the mountains clear? Do you see the valley? Then try it now!' they were told. And so then they came to see everything under heaven and so then they gave thanks to Former and Shaper. [. . .] 'Thanks then to you that we are created, we are formed, we are shaped, we exist O our Grandmother, O our Grandfather.'

"And not very happily did they listen to this, the Former and Shaper. 'It is not good what they said, our forming, our shaping: *We know everything great and small,*' *they said.* And so they took back again their knowledge, did Bearer and Engenderer. 'How shall we make them again so that their sight reaches only nearby? [. . .] Then, so be it! Let's just undo them a little more. That's what is still needed. It isn't good what we have found out. Won't they just equate their deeds with ours if their understanding reaches too far and they see everything?' [. . .]

"And their eyes were chipped by the Heart of Heaven. They were blinded like the clouding of the surface of a mirror; their eyes were all blinded. They could only see nearby then, however clear things might be, and thus they lost their understanding, and all the wisdom of the four men at the start, at the beginning. And thus was the forming, the shaping of our first grandfathers, our first fathers, by the Heart of Heaven, the Heart of Earth. And then there were their mates; and their wives came to exist" (pp. 125–27).

Nicodemos of the Holy Mountain: "The mind rises above this earth, cuts through the air, passes beyond the atmosphere, the planets and all the starry expanse of space, and even beyond the angelic and other-worldly powers. The mind thus goes out and beyond all physical and spiritual things and reasons to envision the unconfused Monad and the indivisible Triad, the first and most pure and most simple

Being, the principle of all principles, the cause of causes; the transcendent and hidden One. [. . .] The mind meditates on God, not only relatively as the creative cause of all, but rather directly and absolutely and in himself—as nature and essence that is unmoved, unchanged, infinite, without beginning, simple, unmixed, indivisible, immortal, inapproachable light, ineffable power, limitless size, transcendent glory, desired goodness, and irresistible beauty that is strongly partaken by the contrite heart, but impossible to express with words" (pp. 213–14).

Richard of St. Victor: "Therefore, essentially He is within all things and outside all things, below all things and above all things. If He is within all things, nothing is more secret than He is. If He is outside all things, nothing is farther away than He is. If He is below all things, nothing is more obscure than He is. What is more incomprehensible than that than which nothing is more secret, nothing farther away, nothing more obscure, nothing more sublime? Again, if He is in every place, nothing is more present than He is. If He is outside every place, nothing is more absent than He is. But is anything more absent than the very One who is the most present of all, and is anything more present than that very One who is the most absent of all, who does not have to be one thing and another in order to be everything that exists? But if nothing is more present than the most absent and nothing is more absent than the most present, what is more marvelous than this, what is more incomprehensible?" (pp. 291–92).

William Law: "There is nothing that so powerfully governs the heart, that so strongly excites us to wise and reasonable actions, as a true sense of God's presence. But as we cannot see or apprehend the essence of God, so nothing will so constantly keep us under a lively sense of the presence of God as this holy resignation which attributes everything to Him and receives everything from Him" (p. 326).

"Therefore, my child, fear and worship and love God. Your eyes indeed cannot yet see Him, but everything you see are so many marks of His power and presence and He is nearer to you than anything you can see" (p. 255).

Johannes Tauler: "To experience the working of the Trinity is better than to talk about it. In fact one shies away from a busy scrutiny of this mystery, especially as the words are borrowed from the world as we know it, and also because of the disproportion between the subject and our intelligence to which all this is unutterable height and hidden. [. . .] Above all, cherish this very sweet Image which dwells in you in such a blessed and unique manner. Nobody can express adequately its nobility, for God is in this Image, indeed He is the Image, in a way which surpasses all our powers of comprehension" (pp. 104–5).

Meister Eckhart: "On what does this true possession of God depend, so that we may truly have him? This true possession of God depends on the disposition, and on an inward directing of the reason and intention toward God, not on a constant contemplation in an unchanging manner, for it would be impossible to nature to preserve such an intention and very laborious, and not the best thing either. A man ought not to have a God who is just a product of his thought, nor should he be satisfied with that, because if the thought vanished, God too would vanish. But one ought to have a God who is present, a God who is far above the notions of men and of all created things. That God does not vanish, if a man does not wilfully turn away from him" (pp. 252–53).

Johannes Tauler: "The soul is [God's] image, the same Image God possesses within His own pure divine Essence. And here, in this Image, God loves and comprehends Himself and rejoices in Himself. He lives and works and has His Being in the soul.

"By this action the soul becomes God-hued, divinized, reformed in the form of God. It possesses everything by grace which God possesses by nature by way of its union with Him and by sinking into Him. Thus the soul soars far above itself, right into the very core of God. So much does the soul take on God's hue that, could it behold itself, it would take itself for God. And whoever would perceive the soul would find it clothed with the divine form, God-hued, by the light of grace; and he would rejoice greatly in it, for in this union God and the soul are one, not by nature but by grace" (p. 128).

7. Body and Spirit

*T*he sixth set of questions inquires about the relationship between body and spirit for the person who is intent on growth in the devout life. "What is the relationship between your body (well or sick, strong or weak) and your spiritual life?" "What is the relationship between yourself as a sexual person and your spiritual life?" As you will see in the readings which follow, even the way in which the two parts of the question are posed betrays a perspective on the relationship between body and spirit. It is not the perspective which has characterized most of the writings in the Classics of Western Spirituality.

Typically there is not a great deal said about the body in the Classics, and much that is said seems to view the body negatively. The indexes of most books do not list the word "body." We found a variety of other words to lead us to an understanding of how authors understood the relationship between body and spirit: bloodletting, chastity, continence, death, dreams, evil thoughts, fasting, Genesis 2:4, heart, male and female, marriage, mortification, senses, sensory pleasure, sensuality, suffering, tears. No index consulted had the word "sex" or "sexual." (The word "sexuality" appeared once under "Interrogations in . . . ," in *Birgitta of Sweden*.) Needless to say, this made the second part of our question difficult to answer!

The world of these authors was very different from the

world of cultural meanings which we share. Indeed, it is clear in reading many of the answers that their meaning could be fully understood only by people inside the culture reflected in the writings. Nevertheless, these texts do give us the opportunity to reflect on some themes which character- ize, in one way or another, much of what has been written about the body within devotional literature and spiritual writings. It may be in this area that we have something partic- ular to share with God's friends. What we can perhaps learn from our own experience is that the articulation of answers to these questions is not easy, and that the culture (rather than faith) dictates much of what we think (or have thought). These are questions which must be answered thoughtfully by all who are concerned with the spiritual life. Given what we know from modern psychology about the pervasiveness of bodiliness and sexuality in the human per- son, we may approach these questions with enthusiasm. Given what we know about the human capacity for self- deception, we may approach these questions (as we do so many others) with a certain wariness.

The answers to these questions did not admit of easy division into the four approaches we have used to this point. Therefore we have made a substantial shift in grouping the texts. We have *not* grouped them by approach in the same way in which we grouped other texts. We have grouped them according to the characteristic approach of each au- thor. Thus, if Julian of Norwich is typically in the Heart/ imaging approach, her quotations are listed in this section under the heading, "Authors usually listed under Heart/ imaging." If Johannes Tauler is typically in the Mind/emp- tying of images approach, his quotations will be listed under the heading, "Authors usually listed under Mind/emptying of images." In most cases, however, there is little or no inter- nal evidence in the text to place it in one or another approach. We have used this system simply to make it easier for you to find favorite authors.

We invite you to spend time now with your own answers. Write them carefully and with attention to your own experience. When you read the quotes which follow, recognize that they represent a very different, and to us almost incomprehensible, cultural world. Where they speak to us, we may listen to them with attention and openness, always claiming our own truth.

Authors usually listed under Heart/imaging

Julian of Norwich: "A man walks upright, and the food in his body is shut up as if in a well-made purse. When the time of his necessity comes, the purse is opened and then shut again, in most seemly fashion. And it is God who does this, as it is shown when he says that he comes down to us in our humblest needs. For he does not despise what he has made, nor does he disdain to serve us in the simplest natural functions of our body, for love of the soul which he created in his own likeness. For as the body is clad in the cloth, and the flesh in the skin, and the bones in the flesh, and the heart in the trunk, so are we, soul and body, clad and enclosed in the goodness of God" (p. 186).

"Our true Mother Jesus, he alone bears us for joy and for endless life, blessed may he be. So he carries us within him in love and travail, until the full time when he wanted to suffer the sharpest thorns and cruel pains that ever were or will be, and at the last he dies. And when he had finished, and had borne us so for bliss, still all this could not satisfy his wonderful love [. . .] for the precious love of motherhood has made him our debtor" (p. 298).

"Also I saw our Lord scorn [the devil's] malice and despise him as nothing, and he wants us to do so. Because of this sight I laughed greatly, and that made those around me laugh as well; and their laughter was pleasing to me. [. . .] I understood that we may laugh, to comfort ourselves and rejoice in God, because the Devil is overcome" (pp. 201–2).

Catherine of Siena: "The truly perfect and obedient [. . .] are patient, strong, and persevering, for those virtues are friends of obedience. They bypass the devil's assaults by mortifying and subduing their flesh, stripping it of delights and pleasures and clothing it in the labors of the order, faithfully and without disdain. Like little ones who do not remember their father's beatings or the hurts inflicted on them, these little ones do not remember any hurts or burdens or beatings they might receive from their superiors in the order. No, when their superiors call them they go back to them humbly, not obsessed with hatred or anger or bitterness, but with meekness and good will" (p. 345).

Symeon the New Theologian: "If you love God genuinely and you also persevere in His love (cf. Jn 15:9, 10), you will never be dominated by any passion, nor will you be reduced to subjection by any necessity of the body. For since the body cannot be moved to anything apart from the soul, so the soul that is united to God by love cannot be led astray to the pleasures and cravings of the body, nor indeed to any other desires of anything visible or invisible, whether desire or passion. For by the sweet love of God the impulse of its heart, or rather, the whole inclination of its will, is bound. When once, as I have said, it has been bound to its Maker, how can it be inflamed by the body or in any way fulfill its own desires? In no way!" (p. 270).

Francis of Assisi: "Similarly, all the brothers should

fast from the feast of All Saints until Christmas, and from the Epiphany, when our Lord Jesus Christ began to fast, until Easter. At other times, however, they are not obliged to fast according to this life except on Fridays. And they may eat whatever food is placed before them, according to the Gospel (cf. Lk 10:8)" (p. 112).

Bonaventure: "Fervently exhorting the friars to observe this rule, Francis used to say that nothing of what he had placed there came from his own efforts but that he dictated everything just as it had been revealed by God. To confirm this with greater certainty by God's own testimony, when only a few days had passed the stigmata of our Lord Jesus were imprinted upon him by the finger of the *living God*" (p. 217).

"[Francis] was ablaze with a great desire to return to the humility he practiced at the beginning, to nurse the lepers as he did at the outset and to treat like a slave once more his body that was already in a state of collapse from his work. [. . .] His body was so much in harmony with his spirit and so ready to obey it that when he strove to attain complete holiness, his body not only did not resist, but even tried to run ahead" (p. 315).

A Winnebago Father's Teachings to His Son (*Native North American Spirituality of the Eastern Woodlands*): "You ought to be of some help to your fellowmen and for that reason I counsel you to fast. Our grandfather who stands in our midst sends forth all kinds of blessings. Try then and obtain one of these. [. . .] If you have not obtained war blessings, fast for your position in life. If you fast in this way, after you get married you will get along well. You will then not have to worry about having children nor about your happiness. [. . .] If you fast often enough for these things, then some day when your children ask for food, they will be able to obtain without difficulty a piece of deer meat, or perhaps even a piece of moose meat. You have it within you to see to it that your children shall never be hungry" (pp. 70–71, 73–74).

The Menominee Puberty Fast (*Native North American Spirituality*): "Long ago in the ancient time our ancestors, the Indians of old, used to have supernatural power, for the spirits took pity on them and blessed them, giving them their help. This was the rite they always performed: They fasted, afflicting their own souls. They ate nothing and drank nothing. Parents made their children fast so that they might therefrom gain a continuance of mortal life. This was what the faster was to get as a blessing from the spirits; this was the thing: He was to see an evil vision or else a good vision; this was what the faster gained, if he was really helped by the spirits. And it was through this that a person succeeded in prolonging and assuring his life. [. . .]

"When a young person began to fast, his body was really clean, as was symbolized by his painting his face with charcoal. And this was why he was able to see a vision, because there was nothing in his stomach. The father, when he arranged his child's fast, would ask him from time to time what sort of vision he had seen. If the faster related an evil vision, then the father would needs tell his son to eat. He did this so that the latter should reject the bad dream" (pp. 84–85).

John Wesley: "Q. But can any one who has a pure heart prefer pleasing to unpleasing food? Or use any pleasure of sense which is not strictly necessary? If so how do they differ from others? A. The difference between these and others in taking pleasant food is (a) They need none of these things to make them happy; for they have a spring of happiness within. They see and love God. [. . .] We answer directly: Such a one may use pleasing food, without the danger which attends those who are not saved from sin. He may prefer it to unpleasing, though equally wholesome, food as a means of increasing thankfulness, with a single eye to God, who gives us all things richly to enjoy. On the same principle, he may smell a flower, or eat a bunch of grapes or take delight in any other pleasure which does not lessen, but increases his delight in God. Therefore neither can we say that one perfected in love would be incapable of marriage, and of worldly business. If he were called thereto, he would be more capable than ever, as being able to do all things without hurry or concern, without any distraction of spirit" (p. 333).

Authors usually listed under Heart/emptying of images

The Cloud of Unknowing: "The same subjection of the body to the spirit can truly be understood, in a sense, in the spiritual exercise described in this book, by the experience of those who undertake it. For whenever a soul disposes itself effectively to this exercise, then straight away and suddenly, and imperceptibly on the part of him who is making the exercise, the body, that perhaps before he began was a little bent over towards one side or the other in order to be more comfortable, comes upright by the power of the spirit, so that the body imitates and follows the work of the spirit, which is happening spiritually; and this is very appropriate" (p. 240).

"The Ancient Word" (*Mesoamerican Spirituality*): "The Lord of the Near and Close has said, you are ordained one woman for one man. However, you are not to ruin yourself impetuously; you are not to devour, to gulp down the carnal life as if you were a dog.

"Especially are you to become courageous, are you yet to become strong, are you yet to reach maturity. Even as the maguey,[1] you are to form a stalk, you are to ripen. Then, thereby, you will become strong in the union, in the marriage your children will be rugged, agile, and they will be polished, beautiful, clean. And well will you enter into your carnal life: In your carnal life you will be rugged, strong, swift; diligent will you be.

"And if you ruin yourself impetuously, if too soon you seduce, you discover women on earth, verily the old men went saying, you will interrupt your development, you will be stunted, your tongue will be white, your mouth will become swollen, puffed . . ." (p. 82).

"At midnight, when, as was said, night divided in half, [all those who were to become fire priests and offering priests] arose; they prayed. If one failed to do so because he slept, if one did not awake, then, for this, there was a gathering together. They drew blood from his ears, his breast, his thighs, the calves of his legs. Verily, because of this, fear descended" (p. 94).

Sharafuddin Maneri: "It is ignorance and foolishness on the part of anyone to think that the Law has enjoined the complete extirpation of desires and other human tendencies! The ideal should not be considered in terms of such extremes. Nothing of that sort is commanded. The Prophet of

---

1. The maguey plant, used to make a spirituous drink, produced liquid for a rather limited span of time once it was tapped.

Islam himself has said, 'I am a man. I get angry.' [. . .] To what extent does he order that there should be no sexual desire? [. . .] If anyone loses this appetite, he should seek treatment to have it restored. [. . .] The sexual appetite and anger are like dogs and horses. Without these two, one cannot go hunting for eternal bliss. The precondition is to bring both to heel. If they gain the upper hand, then they can wreak a man's destruction. The whole purpose of austerities is to break the dominance of these two qualities and place them firmly under control. It is possible to do this" (p. 75).

George Herbert:
Abstain wholly, or wed. Thy bounteous Lord
Allows thee choice of paths: take no byways;
But gladly welcome what he doth afford;
Not grudging, that thy lust hath bounds and stays.
    Continence hath his joy: weigh both; and so
    If rottenness have more, let Heaven go (p. 121).

Yet Lord instruct us to improve our fast
By starving sin and taking such repast,
    As may our faults control:
That ev'ry man may revel at his door,
Not in his parlor; banqueting the poor,
    And among those his soul (p. 206).

Get me a standing there, and place
    Among the beams, which crown the face
        Of him, who died to part
            Sin and my heart (p. 191).

Augustine: "Thus I came to understand by way of personal experience what I had read, how the 'flesh lusts against the spirit, and the spirit against the flesh' (Gal 5:17) [. . .] I was as much afraid of being freed from what hindered my going to you as I should have feared whatever might hinder this. So I was as pleasantly weighed down by the baggage of this world as one often is in sleep. And the thoughts by which I meditated on you were like the struggles of someone desirous to get up and yet overcome by a deep sleep, falling back again into it. [. . .] I was certain that it was better for me to commit myself to your love rather than yield to my sensuality, but although the former course was pleasing and convincing, the latter delighted my body and held it in bondage" (p. 87).

The Zohar: "Come and see: The Blessed Holy One does not place His abode in any place where male and female are not found together. Blessings are found only in a place where male and female are found, as it is written: 'He blessed them and called their name Adam on the day they were created.' It is not written: 'He blessed him and called his name Adam.' A human being is only called Adam when male and female are as one" (p. 56).

Authors usually listed under Mind/imaging

The first text needs a word of explanation. It is a truly wonderful conversation and argument between Body, Soul, and Self-Love, but is too long to reproduce here in any except the most sketchy form. Even this, however, may shed some light on other texts in this chapter, although it does not do justice to the subtlety and humor of Catherine's thought.

Catherine of Genoa: "SOUL: Tell me precisely what are the needs you claim you cannot do without? I will provide for them and in that way no longer be fearful.

"BODY: My needs are food, drink, sleep, dress. That is,

to be served in one way or another so that, in turn, I can serve you. In attending to your spiritual needs, however, do not vex me. When I am disgruntled, I cannot attend to those needs. If God provided so many delightful things for me, the Body, think of what he may have in store for you, the immortal Soul! We can both do homage to God in this manner —and when we have our differences, Self-Love will settle them.

"SOUL: Very well. Since I cannot do otherwise, I will provide for your needs. I am afraid, though, that you are both plotting against me. Your words are so utterly sensible on the surface that they force me to be understanding; yet, I wonder what you have in mind when you insist that without me you can do nothing. [. . .]

"The Soul then said to Self-Love: In meeting your needs, I notice that bit by bit my own convictions are weakening. Are you not getting more than your due? And in following you am I not going to be badly hurt? Indeed not I alone, but all three of us? You are the arbiter. What do you think?

"Self-Love answered: It is because you were aiming so unreasonably high that you feel as if you are debasing yourself to come down to our level. With time, though, you will learn to moderate yourself, to be more sensible. Our company is not so bad as you seem to think at this point. Fear not, God will provide. You are to love God fully, not in this world but in the next." [. . .] As the days passed, however, the Soul lost more and more of its instinct for things divine. [. . .]

"SOUL: In acceding to the desires of the Body, under the guise of necessity—a notion that led straightway to that of the necessity of the superfluous—in a very short time I became enmeshed in sin. I became arid and heavy, a thing of the earth. The appetites and food for the Body and of Self-Love were mine; and you, Self-Love, had so tightly bound yourself to me and the Body that I almost suffocated. [. . .] I sighed with longing, not knowing what it was I sought—and that was the prompting, the instinct for God, that was mine by nature. [. . .]

"On seeing the creature lose all confidence in itself and turn to Him, God comes to his aid. [. . .] He does this in diverse ways, as He sees fit. In this instance we will speak of how He does so with Pure Love" (pp. 91–107).

Jacob Boehme: "The third and most abominable chain by which the poor soul is bound is the corrupted, and completely vain, earthly, mortal flesh and blood, full of evil desires and inclinations" (p. 28).

"Now when Adam and Eve fell into this misery, the anger of nature awoke in each characteristic and impressed in its desire the vanity of the flesh and the anger of God into itself. Then the flesh became gross and harsh, as any other animal, and the noble soul was caught in the essence by it. They looked at themselves, and saw that they were beasts in their bodies and saw their bestial organs for reproduction, and the stinking intestines in which the desires of the flesh enclosed vanity (nausea). They were ashamed of this before God, and they crept under the trees in the Garden of Eden. Heat and cold also fell upon them" (p. 149).

"O sweet Love, You are my light; illuminate my poor soul in its dark prison, in flesh and blood. Lead it continually on the right path. Break the devil's will and lead my body through the course of this world, through death's chamber, into Your death and peace so that on the Last Day it will be resurrected out of Your death into You and live with You eternally. Teach me what I ought to do in You. Be my will, knowledge and activity and do not let me do anything with-

out You. I give myself fully and completely to You. Amen"
(p. 50).

Birgitta of Sweden: "Fourth question. 'Item. Why have
you given men and women sexual organs and the seed for
intercourse if it may not be spilt according to the appetites of
the flesh?'
"Fifth question. 'Item. Why have you given a heart and
a will if not to like that which tastes sweeter and love that
which is more delightful to enjoy?'
"Response to the fourth question. 'Item. I gave seed for
intercourse for this reason: that it might germinate in the
proper way and in the proper place and that it might bear
fruit for a just and rational cause.'
"Response to the fifth question. 'Item. I gave man a
heart so that he might enclose it in me, his God, who am
everywhere and incomprehensible, so that his delight might
be in thinking of me' " (pp. 104–5).

Hildegard of Bingen: "But the first woman's being
formed from man means the joining of wife to husband. And
thus it is to be understood: This union must not be vain or
done in forgetfulness of God, because He Who brought forth
the woman from the man instituted this union honorably
and virtuously, forming flesh from flesh. Wherefore, as
Adam and Eve were one flesh, so now also a man and
woman become one flesh in a union of holy love for the
multiplication of the human race. And therefore there
should be perfect love in these two as there was in those first
two" (pp. 77–78).

Early Dominican Constitutions: "He should teach
them how they are to remain in their rooms, to keep their
eyes lowered, how and what they are to pray and how

quietly they should pray, so that they do not disturb others with their roaring. [. . .] He should teach them that they must use two hands to drink and should only drink sitting down, and how careful they must be with books and clothes and other things belonging to the monastery. He should teach them how earnest they must be in their study, always reading or thinking about something by day and by night, in the house and when they are on a journey, and striving to retain as much as they can in their minds" (p. 466).

"From the Lives of the Sisters" (*Early Dominicans*): "Sister Agnes of Ochsenstein [. . .] led a pure and innocent life from childhood, and kept the flower of her virginity untainted all her life. [. . .] She was a model of holiness, a pattern of religious life, the very image of monastic purity, and exceptionally faithful to the regular observance. [. . .] In addition to this, she was a very gentle and effective comforter of all the sisters, so that anyone who went to her because of any kind of upset always came away consoled. [. . .] She was beyond all comparison in her practice of abstinence. She practiced the utmost moderation in food and drink, mortifying herself most severely for the sake of the Lord; almost all her life she abstained, in things great and small, from any food which might possibly appeal to her appetite, and when the other sisters were eating two dishes at table, she always did without one of them for herself, and she would eat dry barley bread, refusing white bread if she was offered it. She always refused to take even a taste of apples or nuts or other such fruits. Her way of life was very strict and tightly disciplined. She wore down and punished her innocent body most aggressively with vigils and fasts, constant prayers, and with no end of other such good works. [. . .]

"But this was not nearly enough to satisfy the fervor of her spirit, which was always seething with the fire of divine love; she added yet another way of grievously afflicting herself. For many years she tied three different kinds of girdle tightly round herself next to the skin [. . .] After her death, the skin and flesh under these girdles [of iron and rope] was found to be as black as if it had been stained with coal, and we saw that it was all decayed"[2] (pp. 417–18).

"Beginnings of Wisdom" *(Safed Spirituality)*: "The body, which is created from a fetid drop, is a part of this world; its ultimate destiny is destruction, just as every good thing belonging to this world winds up diminished and ruined. This is so because the body derives from the serpent's skin and its evil shell. An individual who pays greater homage to his physical body than he does to his soul is like one who shows greater respect to human beings than he does to the Holy One, blessed be He. [. . .] We do not adorn the soul in the world to come except by means of the soul's 'garment.' This heavenly garment is 'woven' by the body's limbs in the course of their carrying out the commandments. Such garments are lovely, free of the stains of sins and free of all imperfection. In this way, a person draws honor upon his soul. If he is lacking in any one of the commandments, however, his soul experiences no honor" (pp. 130–31).

Authors usually listed under Mind/emptying of images

Origen: "I pray that our souls may never be disquieted, and even more that in the presence of the tribunals and of

---

2. Such forms of self-inflicted penance may seem repugnant to us. Bodily mortifications, including self-flagellation, were common in this period, and reflected an intense desire of many Christians to suffer with Christ and do penance for their sins. In the case of Sister Agnes it is clear that the biographer praises her for her practice of Christian virtue first and foremost.

the naked swords drawn against our necks that they may be guarded by the peace that passes all understanding (cf. Phil 4:7), and may be quieted when they consider that those who are foreigners from the body are at home with the Lord of all (cf. 2 Cor 5:8)." (p. 43).

"Many, conquered by their pains and not knowing how to bear their diseases with courage, disgrace their souls rather than their bodies when they are sick" (p. 154).

Maximus the Confessor: "Of the things given to us by God for our use some are in the soul, others in the body, and others are concerned with the body. [. . .] The good or evil use of these things or those corresponding to them indicates whether we are virtuous or wicked. [. . .]

"In the body there are, for example, pleasure and hardship, feeling and disability, health and illness, life and death, and similar things. Of those things concerned with the body there are, for example, parenthood and childlessness, wealth and poverty, fame and ill repute, and so forth. Some of these we consider good and others evil, although none of them is evil in itself but is found to be properly good or evil according to its use" (pp. 56–57).

"The one who keeps his body away from pleasure and sickness keeps it as a fellow worker in the service of better things" (p. 37).

Johannes Tauler: "Now let us see how we should act initially, when we are about to receive this witness [from Uncreated Light]. We must detach ourselves from everything that is temporal and transitory, for this witness is to be received by the lower and higher faculties within us. The lowest faculty is our appetite for pleasure and the irascible appetite. Hence it is the faculty for pleasure which will first receive this witness, and therefore we must cut ourselves off from all those natural pleasures we find most gratifying: society, fashion, in short anything which satisfies the senses, though God permits us to satisfy our needs. It is indeed a wilderness into which God is taking us: a life of detachment in which we shed our desires, spiritual and natural, in our interior and exterior life" (p. 146).

"[God] wishes to lead our spirit to the very heights—so noble is it—beyond the body, into a spiritual realm. He desires the body to retain its dignity, being practiced in virtue, in trials and rejections, patiently borne. God wills that both spirit and body should hold their proper place, so that they may be reunited in a dignity a thousand times higher, devoid of all fear" (p. 95).

Meister Eckhart (*Essential Sermons*): "But there is something else that should console a man. If he is sick and in great bodily pain, he still has a house and what he needs to eat and drink, doctors to treat him, his servants to look after him, his friends to sympathize and be with him. What more does he want? What do poor people do when they have times when they are as sick or even sicker, and have no one to give them a cup of cold water? They have to go out begging a crust of bread in the rain and the snow and the cold from house to house. So if you want consolation, forget those who are better off and think of all those for whom things are worse" (p. 214).

Gregory Palamas: "For it is the case that if we cannot taste mental prayer, not even as it were with the slightest touch of our lips, and if we are dominated by passionate emotions, then we certainly stand in need of the physical suffering that comes from fasting, vigils and similar things, if we are to apply ourselves to prayer. This suffering alone mortifies the body's inclination to sin, and moderates and weakens the thoughts that provoke violent passions. Moreover, it is this which brings about within us the start of holy compunction, through which both the stain of past faults is done away and the divine favor especially attracted, and which dispose one towards prayer. For 'God will not despise a bruised heart,' as David says; and according to Gregory the Theologian, 'God heals in no more certain way than through suffering.' This is why the Lord taught us in the Gospels that prayer can do great things when combined with fasting" (p. 49).

Martin Luther: "The obligations and rule of this earthly life must be in keeping with an outflow of the true Light. But that which does not represent a 'must' or such an 'ought' but rather flows from sheer egotistic desire cannot be in keeping with the true Light. Man often invents for himself many musts and oughts that are actually false. When he is driven by his pride, avarice, and other vices and also evils of commissions and omission, he declares: 'It must be, it ought to be.' When he is driven by the urge for people's approval and friendship, or by his body's desires in this direction or that, he declares: 'It must be, it ought to be.'

"Look, all this is false. If man had no other must and ought than that which God and the Truth inspire in him, he would often have more truly upbuilding tasks than he has right now" (p. 85).

8. *Community of Faith*

*I*n this section we invite you to turn your attention to your community of faith. Describe the principal features of your community of faith. What is the place of this community of faith in your spiritual life? By "community of faith" we mean many things: your church or synagogue, your present religious tradition, the religious influences which formed you, your place of worship, your religious community, the people with whom you identify in matters of faith, even—should this be the case—the people *against whom* you define your spiritual life.

However close to or distant from a community of faith we may be, and however much our spiritual life is truly personal, we have all *received* our faith in some way; faith is something which is handed on. It is the process and reality of this handing on to which we first direct your attention. To the extent that you have been influenced by others in your spiritual life, try to identify these influences; let your heritage claim you. To the extent that you have defined yourself in opposition to a variety of influences, try to identify precise themes and moments; let your own voice be heard.

Many, perhaps most, of us find ourselves presently supported by a community of faith. Our prayer, our worship, our devotion is in some real way connected to other people. (Even hermits may perceive themselves as living within a "communion of saints.") It is to your present community of faith that we now invite you to turn your attention. How do you describe your present community of faith, and how does this community of faith interact with you? How does it shape or support your spiritual life? What does it ask or demand of you? How important is it to you? How has the relationship between your community of faith and your spiritual life developed and changed over the years?

Once again, we invite you to be caring and careful in your reflections. Do not go too quickly to the quotes which follow. You, too, have an important truth to speak. Write your words with attention and with love. Then, turn to the following texts, beginning where you are comfortable.

You will find a wide range of opinion. No doubt some of the words you read will ring true and some will ring false. The quotes come from a wide range of sources; they represent Muslim, Jewish, and Christian religious traditions; they advocate a variety of patterns of interaction between an individual and a community of faith. We trust that the words of these of God's friends will encourage you, challenge you, strengthen you. We also hope that you will enter into conversation with them.

Heart/imaging

Jane de Chantal: "So, courage, dear ones. May all of you together, and each one in particular, work at this and never grow slack. May you all live in harmony with one heart and mind in God. Do not wish for anything except what your superiors and your Sisters ask of you. Show a childlike trust and gentleness toward one another, supporting each one in mutual charity. Never be astonished at the faults of the community or of any individual Sister, for to be shocked at our Sisters' faults, to pick them apart, examine them, to get all upset about them is the sign of a narrow-mindedness which has no insight into human frailty, and very little charity or forbearance. That is why those who are inclined to be so righteous should close their eyes to what is going on around them and remind themselves constantly that charity does not go looking for evil, and when she does come upon it, she looks the other way and excuses those who commit it. This should be our attitude toward our Sisters who are our companions.

"As regards submission to your superiors, I refer you to the constitution on obedience: there is to be no criticizing of our superiors or censure of the conduct of those whom God has given us. Never let this happen among you, my dearest daughters, for it offends God too much! Be simple and perfectly open toward all. Accept lovingly to be admonished and corrected, and never complain, murmur, or blame others.

"In the name of God, beloved daughters, take my advice, for I speak to you in God's presence and with a most caring, maternal affection" (p. 261).

Symeon the New Theologian: "Guard your strictness toward all even in the examination of each man's thoughts, so that you may know who may stand together with those who pray and communicate, and who should be separated to do penance with tears and stand with the penitents. Beware of being partial and thus knowingly or unknowingly making the Church of God, instead of a holy temple, into a cave of robbers (cf. Mt 21:13) or a house of harlots. For this you will not escape the terrible punishment of God's wrath (cf. Rom 2:3)!" (p. 224).

Catherine of Siena: "I have told you all this to make you shake up the fire of your holy longing and your compassion and grief over the damnation of souls. I want your sorrow and love to drive you to pressure me with sweat and tears—tears of constant humble prayer offered to me in the flames of burning desire. And not just for yourself, but for so many others of my creatures and servants who will hear you and be compelled by my love (together with you and my other servants) to beg and pressure me to be merciful to the world and to the mystic body of holy Church, the Church for which you so earnestly plead with me.

"You will recall that I already told you I would fulfill your desires by giving you refreshment in your labors, that I would satisfy your anguished longings by reforming holy Church through good and holy shepherds. I will do this, as I told you, not through war, not with the sword and violence, but through peace and calm, through my servants' tears and sweat. I have set you as workers in your own and your neighbors' souls and in the mystic body of holy Church. In yourselves you must work at virtue; in your neighbors and in the Church you must work by example and teaching. And you must offer me constant prayer for the Church and for every creature, giving birth to virtue through your neighbors. For I have already told you that every virtue and every sin is realized and intensified through your neighbors. Therefore, I want you to serve your neighbors and in this way save the fruits of your own vineyard" (p. 159).

"O my loved ones! They who were superiors became as subjects. They who were in authority became as servants. Though they were healthy, without the sickness and leprosy of deadly sin, they became as if afflicted. Though they were strong, they became as if weak. With the dull and simple they showed themselves as simple, and with the lowly, as lowly. And so with every sort of person they knew how to deal humbly and with charity, giving to everyone the right food.

"What made this possible? The hungry longing they had conceived in me for my honor and the salvation of souls. They ran to feast on these at the table of the most holy cross, refusing no labor and evading no toil. Zealous as they were for souls and for the welfare of holy Church and the spread of the faith, they walked through the brambles of trial and exposed themselves to every sort of danger with true patience. They offered me the fragrant incense of eager longing and constant humble prayer. With their tears and sweat they anointed the wounds the guilt of deadly sin had made, and those who humbly received this anointing regained perfect health" (pp. 228–29).

Richard Rolle: "The condition of life in which you live, in other words, solitude, is the most suitable of all for the revelation of the Holy Spirit. For example, it was when Saint John was on the Isle of Patmos that God revealed to him his secrets. This is the special goodness of God that he should encourage miraculously those who have no encouragement from the world. If they give their hearts entirely to him and desire nothing, and look for nothing except himself, then he gives himself in sweetness and delight, in the ardor of love, and in pleasure and music, and remains constantly with them in spirit so that his strength never leaves them" (p. 158).

"This degree of love is called the contemplative life, which loves to be solitary, without ringing bells or noise or singing or shouting" (p. 139).

"The Devotion" (*Devotio Moderna*): "These are the customs of our house, the practices kept there and diligently observed by our predecessors, so as to promote peace, harmony, and progress in the spiritual life among ourselves and our successors. [. . .] Faithful people founded and endowed our house so that devout men, priests, and clerics might live in common, leading a modest life supported by the work of their own hands [. . .]; that they might together devoutly frequent churches, reverently obey their prelates and curates, wear humble and simple garb suitable to the clerical estate, diligently observe the canons and decrees of the holy fathers, zealously persist in the exercise of the virtues and of devotion, and show themselves examples to others beyond reproof. We seek in this way to offer God a pleasing and acceptable service, not only through our own upright way of life but also by the conversion and salvation of others whose hearts are moved to remorse by our warnings and example" (p. 155).

John Wesley: "Likewise if you would avoid schism, observe every rule of the Society, and of the bands, for conscience sake. Never omit your class or band; never absent yourself from any public meeting. These are the very sinews of our Society; and whatever weakens, or tends to weaken our regard for these, or our exactness in attending them, strikes at the very root of our community. As one says, 'That part of our economy, the private weekly meetings for prayer, examination, and particular exhortation, has been the greatest means of deepening and confirming every blessing that was received by the word preached, and of diffusing it to others who could not attend the public ministry; whereas, without this religious connection and intercourse, the most ardent attempts by mere preaching have proved of no lasting use' " (p. 365).

Head of thy church, whose Spirit fills,
    And flows through every faithful soul

Unites in mystic love, and seals
Them one, and sanctifies the whole

Less than the least of saints, I join
My littleness of faith to theirs;
O King of all, thine ear incline,
Accept our much availing prayers. (p. 208)

Heart/emptying of images

The final text of this section, that of Fakhruddin ʿIraqi, is extraordinarily image-rich. Why then was it not placed in the previous section? We decided, after some hesitation, to place it here as it seems that the author uses images precisely to show the futility of all images or representations. Thus he uses images to empty of images. The reader may decide differently.

Thomas R. Kelly (*Quaker Spirituality*): "I believe that the group mysticism of the gathered meeting rests upon the Real Presence of God in our midst. Quakers generally hold to a belief in Real Presence, as firm and solid as the belief of Roman Catholics in the Real Presence in the host, the bread and the wine of the Mass. In the host the Roman Catholic is convinced that the literal, substantial Body of Christ is present. For him the Mass is not a mere symbol, a dramatizing of some figurative relationship of man to God. It rests upon the persuasion that an Existence, a Life, the Body of Christ, is really present and entering into the body of man. Here the Quaker is very near the Roman Catholic. For the Real Presence of the gathered meeting is an existential fact. To use philosophical language, it is an ontological matter, not merely a psychological matter. The bond of union in divine fellowship is existential and real, not figurative. It is the life of God himself, within whose life we live and move and have our being. And the gathered meeting is a special case of holy fellowship of the blessed community.

"One condition for such a group experience seems to be this: some individuals need already, upon entering the meeting, to be gathered deep in the spirit of worship. There must be some kindled hearts when the meeting begins. In them, and from them, begins the work of worship. The spiritual devotion of a few persons, silently deep in active adoration, is needed to kindle the rest, to help those others who enter the service with tangled, harried, distraught thoughts to be melted and quieted and released and made plain, ready for the work of God and his Real Presence.

"In power and labor one lifts the group, in inward prayer, high before the throne. With work of soul the kindled praying worshiper holds the group, his comrades and himself, high above the sordid and trivial, and prays in quiet offering that Light may drive away the shadows of self-will. Where this inward work of upholding prayer is wholly absent, I am not sure that a gathered meeting is at all likely to follow" (p. 313).

The Cloud of Unknowing: "For just as when a limb of our body feels sore, all the other limbs are in pain and ill-affected on that account, or when one limb is in good health, all the rest are likewise in good health; so it is, spiritually, with all the limbs of holy Church. For Christ is our Head and we are the limbs, as long as we are in charity" (p. 172).

"You see, my friend, all these works, words and looks that passed between our Lord and these two sisters are given as an example of all actives and all contemplatives that have lived in holy Church since that time, and shall live, until the day of judgment. For Mary stands for all contemplatives, who should conform their behavior to hers; and in the same way Martha stands for the actives, according to the same comparison" (p. 158).

Hadewijch: "On a certain Pentecost Sunday I had a vision at dawn. Matins were being sung in the church, and I was present. My heart and my veins and all my limbs trembled and quivered with eager desire and [. . .] my mind was beset so fearfully and so painfully by desirous love that all my separate limbs threatened to break, and all my separate veins were in travail" (p. 280).

For Holy Church proclaims to us—
Her lofty, her lowly, her priests, her scholars—
That Love is of the highest works
    And the noblest by nature:
Even though she conquers us, she conquers all strength,
    And her power shall last (p. 182).

He who is ready to seize high expectation,
Shall with high expectation seize
    Love with Love's service,
And so with storm take his stand
And stand persistent against Love
    And become equally strong,
    As closely as I can estimate.
    It is to this that Holy Church invites
    All who are docile to her.
    May God now come to our assistance!

He who holds back anything in his heart
Cannot attain to the full growth of love.

One must dare to fight all love with love
If Love is to be contented.
But no one can effect this
With all the service of Holy Church:
He needs to give himself up completely in Love,
And live far from all joys,
And seek support in no emotional pleasure,
And continually search for what is never to be had—
Being glad not to spare
Deeds of love, or storm, or disquiet,
For the sake of Love's dignity.
The Book of Wisdom says this:
Glorious fruit shall he know
Who suffers much for the sake of glorifying Love.

Fakhruddin ʿIraqi:
I have seen that the lane of piety stretches out,
        far, far into the distance;
My dearest friends, can you not show me then
        the way of the madman?
Bring me a glass of Magian wine
        that I may drink deep
for I have given up all thought
        of ascetic piety;
or if the pure wine has all been downed
        bring me the cloudy dregs
for thick residue lights up the heart
        and illuminates the eyes.
Tuppence for the Sufi meeting house!
        I flee the company of the righteous;
fill up a row of glasses with wine
        and bring me the first.
I have no rules or regulations,
        nor heart nor religion—

only I remain, and you, sitting in the corner,
    and the wealth of Poverty.
All fear of God, all self-denial I deny;
    bring wine, nothing but wine
for in all sincerity I repent
    my worship which is but hypocrisy.
Yes, bring me wine, for I have
    renounced all renunciation
and all my vaunted self-righteousness
    seems to me but swagger and self-display.
Now for a time let my proof be wine
    against the sorrow of Time
for only in drunkenness can one be free
    of the hour's grief.
Once I am thoroughly drunk, what difference
    if I end up in a church or in Mecca?
Once I've abandoned myself, what matter
    if I win Union—or separation?
I've been to the gambling house and seen
    that the losers there are pure;
I've been to the monastery and have found
    no one but hypocrites.
Now I've broken my repentance, at least
    do not break our covenant:
at least welcome this broken heart and say
    "How are you? Where have you been?"
I've been to Mecca, to circle the Kaaba
    but they refused me entrance
saying "Off with you! What merit have you earned
    outside, that we should admit you within?"
Then, last night, I knocked
    at the tavern door;
from within came a voice: " ʿIraqi! Come in!
    for you are one of the chosen!"

Mind/imaging

John Donne: "This place then where we take our de-
grees in this knowledge of God, our academy, our university
for that, is the Church. For [. . .] the ordinary place for illumination in the knowledge of God is the Church. [. . .]

" 'Upon this Rock I will build my Church, and the gates
of hell shall not prevail against it.' Therein is denoted the
strength and stability of the Church in itself, and then the
power and authority of the Church upon others. [. . .] We are
forbidden private conventicles, private spirits, private opinions, for, as St. Augustine says well [. . .] If a wall stand
single, not joined to any other wall [. . .] one wall makes not a
house; one opinion makes not catholic doctrine, one man
makes not a Church. For this knowledge of God, the Church
is our academy; there we must be bred and there we may be
bred all our lives and yet learn nothing. Therefore, as we
must be there, so there we must use the means, and the
means in the church are the Ordinances, and institutions of
the Church" (pp. 142–43).

Jacob Boehme: "A proper Christian brings his holy
church along into the congregation. His heart is the true
church where man practices the worship of God. [. . .] Here
the scorner will say that I despise the stone church where the
congregation comes together. To this I say, 'No' " (p. 163).

"The godless man hears what the external soul preaches
to the external world. He takes it as a history. If there is
stubble or straw in the sermon, then he sucks vanity out of it,
and the soul sucks false poison and murder of the devil out
of it. With this it tickles itself, in that it hears how it can direct
mankind. If the preacher is also dead, and sows poison and
insults out of his affects, the devil teaches and the devil

hears. This same teaching is taken by the godless hearts and brings forth wicked fruit out of which the world has become a murder-den of devils so that both in the teacher and hearer there is nothing but vain scorn, slanders, haughtiness, word arguments and antagonism about what is in the husks" (p. 162).

Abraham Isaac Kook: "The psychic life of the individual in its various expressions merges with the larger psychic life through bridges that link them—the heroic personalities of the spiritual life and the psychic treasures of the group. This merger determines the distinctive characteristics of communities, such as societies, families and nations, reaching out to the highest levels of being. The spiritual splendor then descends from the highest spiritual source to the particular units of existence, which are differentiated from the whole only through the limitations of subjectivity. These limitations give way as the morning clouds before the rising sun, through the perception of the universal aspect of existence in every soul and spirit" (pp. 287–88).

"Rules of Mystical Piety" (*Safed Spirituality*): "18. The pious are careful to pray with the congregation in the evening, morning, and afternoon.

"19. One ought to be among the first ten persons at the synagogue for worship in the morning as well as in the evening" (p. 44).

"Beginning of Wisdom" (*Safed Spirituality*): "In addition, to the extent possible, a person must attend the synagogue regularly, whether in order to pray or to study the Torah. For one who attends the synagogue is regarded as an individual who fears the Lord, as Scripture says: 'Who is among you that feareth the Lord, that obeyeth the voice of

His servant? Though he walketh in darkness, and hath no light, let him trust in the name of the Lord, and stay upon his God' (Is 50:10). This verse is also understood to refer to a man who normally attends the synagogue on a regular basis, and fails to attend one day" (p. 133).

Augustine of Hippo: " 'Gathered together in one' refers to the one spirit and one body of which the head is Christ (Col 1:18; Eph 1:22). Such a gathering together is the building of the temple of God; such a gathering together is not accomplished by carnal birth, but by spiritual rebirth.

"Consequently, God dwells within each one singly as in His temples, and in all of them gathered together as in His temple. As long as this temple, like Noah's Ark, is storm-tossed in this world, there is verified the words of the Psalm: 'The Lord dwells in the flood' (Ps 28:10)." (p. 423).

Hildegard of Bingen: "For when the Church, as mentioned, suddenly increased in strong and blessed virtues, by the inspiration of the Holy Spirit the mystical altars were sanctified by the deep longings of the faithful, as is clearly shown to you. And the Church, with steady purpose, turns her footsteps there by example and devotedly offers her dowry, which is the body and blood of the Son of God, to the Creator of all in humble obedience, in the presence of those living and burning lights who are the citizens of Heaven. Why is this? Because as the flesh of My Only-Begotten came into being in the pure womb of the Virgin Mary, and then was delivered up for human salvation, so now His flesh, augmented by the incorrupt purity of the Church, is often given to sanctify the faithful" (p. 240).

"The Church has not yet come to the direction and status she will have; but, with great diligence and industry, she incessantly hastens toward her full beauty through swiftly passing time and by means of her children" (p. 456).

"The Church is not yet perfect in her members and her children; but on the last day, when the number of the elect is filled up, the Church will also be full. And on the last day the whole world will be confounded; I, God, will take away the four elements and all that is mortal in human flesh, and in the consummation of the world there will be full joy for the offspring of the Church" (p. 500).

John Eudes: "If we consider the church of God in the light of faith, we will see that since Jesus Christ is its head and the Holy Spirit is its guide, it cannot in any way wander from the truth or become lost in falsehood. Thus all the ceremonies, customs and functions of the church have been most divinely instituted. Everything it prohibits and commands is most legitimately prohibited and commanded. Everything it teaches is infallibly true. Therefore, we should be ready to die a thousand times rather than stray in the least from the truths it proclaims to us. Thus we must revere and honor, in a special way, everything in the church as holy and sacred" (p. 299).

Savonarola (*Apocalyptic Spirituality*): "Immediately the vision vanished and this word came to me: 'Son, if sinners had eyes they would certainly see how hard and difficult this plague and sharp this sword can be.' The Spirit said that the hard plague and sharp sword signified the rule of evil prelates and those who preach human philosophy. They neither enter the Kingdom of Heaven nor allow others to enter. By this he indicated that the Church had fallen so far because their spiritual attack was much worse than any corporeal tribulations that could happen" (p. 201).

Humbert of Romans: "Sometimes preaching is lacking because of a deficiency on the part of the church's leaders [. . .] either because they are ignorant or because they are engaged in other, less important, tasks and have no time to preach, or because they are devoid of any zeal for souls and so take no interest in preaching.

"Sometimes there is no preaching because it is actually prevented by the church's leaders. There are many prelates who not only do not preach, but also stop others from doing so, who would have been able to preach quite satisfactorily. 'They kept your holy children shut up, through whom the incorruptible light of your law was beginning to be given to the world' (Wisdom 18:4). Preachers are shut up when they are not allowed to preach freely" (p. 264).

Mind/emptying of images

There are texts in this section which we have placed here more because their authors usually use this approach (mind/emptying of images) than because the approach is clearly evident in the texts themselves. Once again we trust readers to judge and use these texts as best suits them.

Anna Mathewson (*The Shakers*): "While Mother Ann and the Elders were at Asa Bacon's, in Ashfield, a number of the Believers were there one evening, and there appeared very extraordinary Northern Lights. One said, 'It is the sign of the coming of the Son of Man in the clouds of heaven.' Mother replied, 'Those signs which appear in the sky are *not* the sign of his coming; but the Second Appearing of Christ is in his Church; and Christ is come to put away sin from his people, and this is the Cloud [of witnesses] alluded to' " (p. 47).

The Shaker Manifesto: "Are the churches of to-day ready for the advent of the Christ? Are they ready to welcome the Jesus of old, renewed in all the glory and power of the heavens, to introduce his humble testimony, of CELIBACY for the kingdom's sake on earth? Are they ready to equalize all their members, after the pattern, when 'all who believe are together, and none possesses aught he or she calls her or his own? When none are MARRIED? When no one says this or that is *mine?* When peace and quietness reign?'

"Such is the Church of Christ, and such is to be the grand church of the future, in vaster numbers than ever were counted! And what will bring about this grand evolution? Simply, the overwhelming conviction that in the absence of Christ, the self-denials of the same Christ have been wanting. Simply, that until those same denials are inaugurated, the Church of Christ cannot be again established" (pp. 171–72).

Gregory Palamas: "But, after having testified to his vision of Christ's glory on the holy mountain—of a light which illumines, strange though it may be, the ears themselves (for they contemplated also a luminous cloud from which the words reverberated)—Peter goes on to say, 'This confirms the prophetic word.' What is this prophetic word which the vision of light confirms for you, O contemplators of God? What if not that verse that God 'wraps Himself in light as in a mantle'? He continues, 'You would do well to pay attention to that prophetic word, as a lamp which shines in a dark place till the day dawns.' What day, if not that which dawned in Thabor? 'Let the morning star arise!' What star, if not that which illuminated Peter there, and also James and John? And where will that star rise, but 'in your hearts'?

"Do you not see how this light shines even now in the hearts of the faithful and perfect?" (pp. 62–63).

Maximus Confessor: "Now that blessed old man used to say that at the first level of contemplation holy Church bears the imprint and image of God since it has the same activity as he does by imitation and in figure. For God who made and brought into existence all things by his infinite power contains, gathers, and limits them and in his Providence binds both intelligible and sensible beings to himself and to one another. Maintaining about himself as cause, beginning, and end all beings which are by nature distinct from one another, he makes them converge in each other by the singular force of their relationship to him as origin. [. . .]

"It is in this way that the holy Church of God will be shown to be working for us the same effects as God, in the same way as the image reflects its archetype. For numerous and of almost infinite number are the men, women, and children who are distinct from one another and vastly different by birth and appearance, by nationality and language, by customs and age, by opinions and skills, by manners and habits, by pursuits and studies, and still again by reputation, fortune, characteristics, and connections: All are born into the Church and through it are reborn and recreated in the Spirit. To all in equal measure it gives and bestows one divine form and designation [. . .]. In accordance with faith it gives to all a single, simple, whole, and indivisible condition which does not allow us to bring to mind the existence of the myriads of differences among them, even if they do exist, through the universal relationship and union of all things with it. It is through it that absolutely no one at all is in himself separated from the community since everyone converges with all the rest and joins together with them by the one, simple, and indivisible grace and power of faith" (pp. 186–87).

Johannes Tauler: " 'And the whole house was filled.'

God fulfills wholly. Wherever He enters, He fills the entire capacity of the soul completely, every nook and corner. [. . .]

"The house where the disciples were gathered was completely filled. In one sense this house signifies Holy Church, which is indeed God's dwelling place. In another sense it signifies each man in whom the Holy Spirit dwells" (p. 92).

With the faith-filled words of Johannes Tauler, friend of God, we end this chapter: "God fulfills wholly. Wherever [God] enters, [God] fills the entire capacity of the soul, completely, every nook and corner." This book is not finished, though, until you have added your words, your voice, your truth. You, too, are God's friend.

Appendix A
Questions about
the Spiritual Life

*W*e present here two sets of questions about the spiritual life. The first is the set that evolved in the course of this project; the second is an earlier set which Henry Simmons proposed about ten years ago; it guided our initial efforts. We present both sets to encourage readers to think through for themselves what questions are important to the articulation of the spiritual life. Neither list is complete. It has been pointed out to us, for example, that questions of mortality and the afterlife are not addressed. No doubt there are many other issues missed! These questions are intended to help you grasp some of the features of *your* spirituality; it is important that you appropriate them as your own.

Set A

The word "spirituality" is used to describe an **orientation** in one's approach to God. It presupposes that other orientations are also valid. The following questions will help you grasp what is your spirituality. There are no right and wrong answers, although some answers will be more complete than others, and some elements will be more or less integrated into the whole.

(1) Is your approach to God more a matter of the heart or of the mind?

(2) What is the relationship between the love of God and the love of neighbor?

(3) What is prayer? Where and when do you best pray? What is the importance of prayer? What is the result or effect of prayer?

(4) Where is the presence of God to be found? How do you know? What is the presence of God like? What if any images of God are helpful to you?

(5) What is the relationship between you and God? What is the relationship between God and you? What is God like?

(6) Describe the principal features of your community of faith. What is the place of this community in your spiritual life?

(7) What is the relationship between your human nature and God's grace? At core, what does it mean to be human and how does God's grace relate to this?

(8) How do you order your day, your week, your life so that your use of time matches what you think about your relationship to God?

(9) What is the relationship between what you do (work, recreation, being with others, forgiving, voting, etc.) and your spirituality?

(10) What is sin?

(11) Describe the relationship between your body (well or sick, strong or weak) and your spiritual life. Describe the relationship between yourself as a sexual person and your spiritual life.

(12) How do you educate yourself about the spiritual life

(reading, discussion with an individual, with a group, TV, etc.)? How do you know what is best for your spiritual growth? Do people ever ask you for spiritual advice?

Set B

The word "spirituality" is used to describe an **orientation** in one's approach to God. It presupposes that other orientations are also valid. The following questions will help you grasp what is your spirituality. There are no right and wrong answers, although some answers will be more complete than others, and some elements will be more or less integrated into the whole.

(1) Where is the presence of God to be found? How do you know? What is the presence of God like?
(2) We **are** our community. Describe the principal features of the community of faith which is yours.
(3) What is the place given to liturgy and sacraments? To preaching? To worship?
(4) What is prayer? Where and when do you best pray? How do you know it is best? To whom do you pray?
(5) What three or four theological principles are most central to your spirituality? What is your most important theological starting point?
(6) Is knowing God more a matter of the heart or of the mind? Describe the elements that are important to you.
(7) Do you know God by dwelling in images or emptying yourself of images? Describe the images that are important to you.
(8) Are female images of God important to you? Explain.
(9) Describe the forms of asceticism (discipline of life) you practice. Why these? What do they accomplish?

(10) We **are** our bodies. Describe the relationship between your body and your spiritual life. What is the relationship between yourself as a sexual person and your spiritual life?

(11) Name (if you can) a "founding event" for your present spirituality. (A "founding event" is some critical event in your life which forever shapes how your world is now understood.)

(12) Describe the relationship between your spirituality and your ethical actions.

(13) Describe the relationship between your spirituality and the political sphere.

(14) What is spiritual guidance for you? What is its necessity?

(15) What persons and/or authors have been important in the development of your spirituality?

(16) Describe changes in your spirituality during the past year or two. What has influenced these changes?

(17) What is sin?

(18) What is the place of labor and of leisure in your spiritual life?

(19) What is the correlation between your spirituality, your theology, and your discipline of life?

(20) What do you foresee as the principal changes in your spirituality over the next few years? What will influence these changes?

Appendix B
Biographical Information

*T*he following persons and works are listed in alphabetical order as their names appear in the *Library of Congress Name Authority* unless otherwise noted. The name under which a person or work is listed comes first, followed by other names. For example, Thomas Aquinas is listed as Thomas Aquinas; Robert Bellarmine is listed as Bellarmine, Robert; and Menachem Nahum of Chernobyl is listed as Nahum, Menachem, of Chernobyl.

Biographical information is taken from the introduction of the various texts in The Classics of Western Spirituality,[1] which readers are most warmly encouraged to consult. Where an author is one of many in a volume, only dates (if available) and identification of source are listed.

"Ancient Word, The." In *Native Mesoamerican Spirituality*.

Angelus Silesius, 1624–1677, German mystic, physician, theologian, poet and priest. Born Johann Scheffler, he used the name Angelus Silesius for his mystical writings and

---

1. New York: Paulist Press. All quotations and texts are from this series.

poetry after he converted from Lutheranism to Roman Catholicism in 1653. *The Cherubic Wanderer* is a series of epigrams.

Arndt, Johann, 1555–1621, German Lutheran theologian, pastor, and author of devotional literature. Considered by some to be a prophet of interior Protestantism. The selections are taken from his *True Christianity*, written in 1606.

Augustine of Hippo, 354–430, Bishop of Hippo, theologian, founder of the Christian tradition of the West. Quotations are taken from *Selected Writings*.

Bellarmine, Robert, 1542–1621, bishop, cardinal, and member of the Society of Jesus, widely recognized for his writings against the Protestants, and less known for his writings on the spiritual life. Selections are taken from *Spiritual Writings*.

Bernard of Clairvaux, 1090–1153, the most influential member of the Cistercian Order, whose monks aspired to live a simple life according to the Rule of St. Benedict. Texts quoted are from *Selected Works* which includes treatises, sermons, and letters.

Birgitta of Sweden, c. 1302–1373, visionary, reformer, foundress. After the death of her husband she went to Rome where she worked for the restoration of the papacy in Rome. She was first abbess of the Order of the Most Holy Savior, an order which became one of the most influential of medieval times in the northern countries. *Life and Selected Revelations* includes her life, the fifth and seventh books of revelations, and four prayers.

Boehme, Jacob, 1575–1624, German mystic, brilliant self-taught person, and cobbler. His *The Way to Christ*, from which quotations are taken, is a collection of nine treatises which serve as a guide to meditation.

Bonaventure, 1217–1274, theologian, professor at the University of Paris, cardinal and adviser to popes, minister general of the Franciscan Order, author of one of the richest syntheses of Christian spirituality of the high Middle Ages. Selections are taken from *Bonaventure: The Soul's Journey into God. The Tree of Life. The Life of St. Francis.*

Cassian, John, c. 365–c. 435, monk, teacher, traveller, founder of a house for monks in Marseilles and another house for nuns. Selections are from his *Conferences.*

Catherine of Genoa, 1447–1510, a married lay woman, a mystic, a humanitarian, and a reformer of the Church. Selections are from *Purgation and Purgatory, The Spiritual Dialogue.*

Catherine of Siena, 1347–1380, affiliate of the Order of Saint Dominic, mystic, humanitarian, reformer, and foundress of a women's monastery of strict observance. Selections are taken from *The Dialogue.*

Chantal, Jane de,[3] 1572–1641, of France, wife and mother, widow, co-foundress of the Visitation of Holy Mary. She was a spiritual leader in her day, and with Francis de

---

3. LIBRARY OF CONGRESS NAME AUTHORITY: Chantal, Jeanne de.

Sales founded a school of spirituality (called Salesian) which centers on the person of Jesus. Selections are taken from her letters: *Francis de Sales, Jane de Chantal: Letters of Spiritual Direction.*

Clare of Assisi, c. 1193–1253, foundress of the monastery of the Poor Ladies of Damiano, a religious community in the spiritual tradition of Francis of Assisi. *Francis and Clare: The Complete Works,* from which selections are taken, includes "The Rule of Saint Clare" and several letters.

Cloud of Unknowing, The. Anonymous work in the English School of Spirituality. *The Cloud of Unknowing* is a late fourteenth-century essay addressed to Christians convinced that God was calling them to a life of solitude. Possibly written by a Carthusian recluse of The East Midlands, England.

de Graw, Hamilton. In *The Shakers: Two Centuries of Spiritual Reflection.*

Devotio Moderna. The *Devotio Moderna* or Modern Devotion was a movement which lasted for a century and a half and reached its high point at the end of the fifteenth century. It spread from The Netherlands to Germany, Belgium, France and Switzerland. It had as a common thrust a search for new ways of meditation for the working class, whether in or outside monasteries. Selections are taken from "The Devotion" (a collection of texts) in *Devotio Moderna: Basic Writings.*

Donne, John, 1572–1631, priest, theologian, preacher, poet, Dean of St. Paul's Cathedral, London. Son of a devout Roman Catholic mother, he became an Anglican and embraced a moderately high-church tradition in opposition to the Puritans. Quotations are taken from *John Donne: Selections from Divine Poems, Sermons, Devotions, and Prayers.*

"Early Dominican Constitutions, The." In *Early Dominicans: Selected Writings.*

Eckhart, Meister, c. 1260–1329, Dominican theologian, prior, and preacher. A papal condemnation of his works (which condemnation was unsound, at least in part, and based on an imperfect knowledge of the fathers of the church) was published after his death. Quotations are taken from *Meister Eckhart* and *Meister Eckhart: Teacher and Preacher.*

Ephrem the Syrian, died in 373 in Edessa while helping victims of the plague. A teacher, writer of hymns, homilies and commentaries, deacon, and founder of a school of biblical and theological studies and women's choirs to sing his hymns, he is the foremost writer in the Syriac tradition of Christianity. Quotations are taken from *Ephrem the Syrian: Hymns.*

Eudes, John, 1601–80, of the French School of spirituality, priest, missionary, seminary reformer. Essays in *Bérulle and the French School: Selected Writings* include "The Life and Kingdom of Jesus in Christian Souls" and "The Most Admirable Heart of the Most Sacred Mother of God."

Francis of Assisi, c. 1182–1226, also known as the Poor Man of Assisi, itinerant preacher and founder of the Order of Friars Minor. *Francis and Clare: The Complete Works* includes letters, blessings, Rules, and prayers.

Francisco de Osuna, c. 1492–c. 1540, Spanish mystic, Franciscan priest, preacher, writer. Quotations are from his *The Third Spiritual Alphabet.*

Hadewijch, 13th-century Flemish mystic, a member of the Beguines, leader of a small contemplative group, and the most important exponent of love mysticism. Quotations are taken from *Hadewijch: The Complete Works.*

Herbert, George, 1593–1633, English aristocrat, parish priest of the Anglican Church in Fuggleston St. Peter, poet. Quotations are taken from his poetry in *George Herbert: The Country Parson, The Temple.*

Hildegard of Bingen, 1098–1179, visionary, founder and first abbess of the Benedictine community at Bingen, theologian, encyclopedist, public preacher, reformer. Quotations are taken from *Hildegard of Bingen: Scivias.*

Humbert of Romans, c. 1200–1277, Dominican. Elected Master of the Order in 1254, he drew together and consolidated the essential structures of the order. His "Treatise on the Formation of Preachers" is found in *Early Dominicans: Selected Writings.*

`Iraqi, Fakhruddin, lived in the 13th century at the peak of the revival in Islamic spirituality. One of the greatest of Persian poets, a Sufi gnostic who spoke in the language of love. Quotations are from *Fakhruddin `Iraqi: Divine Flashes.*

Jacopone da Todi, c. 1236–1306, Franciscan, spiritual master, poet, whose writings are a prototype of intense Italian peasant piety. Quotations are taken from *Jacopone da Todi: The Lauds.*

John of the Cross, 1542–1591, Spanish Carmelite, mystic, reformer, writer. Quotations are from *Selected Writings.*

Jones, Rufus M., 1863–1948. In *Quaker Spirituality: Selected Writings.*

Julian of Norwich, born c. 1343, a woman mystic of the English School of spirituality, she received a series of revelations ("showings") on May 13, 1373. She was a recluse and spiritual guide. Quotations are taken from *Julian of Norwich: Showings.*

Kelly, Thomas R., 1893–1941. In *Quaker Spirituality: Selected Writings.*

Kook, Abraham Isaac, 1865–1935, Latvian Jew, philosopher, mystic, Kabbalist, Rabbinic scholar, utopianist. He served as Rabbi in Lithuania, Jaffa, Palestine, London, and as chief Rabbi in Jerusalem. Quotations are taken from *Abraham Isaac Kook: The Lights of Penitence, Light of Holiness, The Moral Principles, Essays, Letters, Poems.*

Law, William, 1686–1761, a Nonjuring clergyman (and thus unable to hold any university or church appointment), he earned his living as a tutor, private chaplain, and author of devotional texts. Quotations are taken from *William Law: A Serious Call to a Devout and Holy Life. The Spirit of Love.*

León, Luis de, c. 1527–1591, Spanish Augustinian, humanist and intellectual, philosopher, theologian, teacher, and survivor of the Inquisition. Quotations are from *Luis de Leon: The Names of Christ.*

"Lives of the Sisters." In *Early Dominicans: Selected Writings,* "The Dominican Family."

Luther, Martin, 1483–1546, German reformer, theologian, leader of the Protestant revolt against the Church of Rome, and builder of a new church. Quotations are taken from *The Theologia Germanica of Martin Luther.*

Maneri, Sharafuddin, 1263–1381, Sufi mystic of Islamic India. Selections are from *Sharafuddin Maneri: The Hundred Letters.*

Mathewson, Anna. In *The Shakers: Two Centuries of Spiritual Reflection.*

Maximus Confessor, 580–662, monk and spiritual master, student and contemplator of the incarnation, exiled and mutilated for holding the doctrine of the Council of Chalcedon that Christ has a truly human will. Quotations are from *Maximus Confessor: Selected Writings.*

"Menominee Puberty Fast, The." In *Native North American Spirituality of the Eastern Woodlands.*

Nahum, Menachem, of Chernobyl, 1730–1797, Hasidic preacher and scholar of this popular movement of mystical piety. Selections are taken from *Menachem Nahum of Chernobyl: Upright Practices, The Light of the Eyes.*

Nicodemos of the Holy Mountain, 1749–1809, Orthodox Christian, monk of the Holy Mountain Athos, educator for the reform and renewal of the people of the Orthodox Church. Selections are from his *Handbook of Spiritual Counsel.*

Olier, Jean-Jacques, 1608–1680, of the French School of spirituality, priest, known for his work of ecclesial and priestly renewal. Essays in *Selected Writings* include "Introduction to the Christian Life and Virtues" and "The Christian Day."

Origen, 185–250, martyr under Decius, philosopher and churchman, Platonist, theologian of the *Logos* (Word). Quotations are from *Origen: An Exhortation to Martyrdom, Prayer and Selected Works.*

Palamas, Gregory, 1296–1359, major spiritual and intellectual figure of Orthodox Byzantium, monk, archbishop, theologian, and hesychist (one who practices sacred quietude). Quotations are from *The Triads.*

Pennington, John, 1616–1679. In *Quaker Spirituality: Selected Writings.*

Philo of Alexandria, c. 20 B.C.E.–50 C.E., scholar, member of the Jewish-Alexandrian community, synthesizer of Jewish and Hellenistic thought patterns, Platonist and lover of Jewish tradition. Selections are taken from *Philo of Alexandria: The Contemplative Life, The Giants, and Selections.*

"Popol Vuh, The." In *Native Mesoamerican Spirituality,* Part Two, "Creation Myths."

Pseudo-Dionysius, *The Complete Works.* Writings attached to the name of Dionysius the Areopagite (cf. Acts 17:34). Actually Greek works of the fifth or sixth century.

Pursuit of Wisdom, The. Anonymous, 14th century, of the English School of spirituality. By the same author as *The Cloud of Unknowing,* possibly a Carthusian recluse in the East Midlands, England.

Richard of St. Victor, d. 1173, monk and later prior of the Abbey of St. Victor, major spiritual writer, master of contemplation (mysticism). Quotations are from *Richard of St. Victor: The Twelve Patriarchs. The Mystical Ark. Book Three of the Trinity.*

Rolle, Richard, c. 1300–1349, hermit in rural Yorkshire, spiritual guide, author of devotional texts for women, of the English School of spirituality. Selections are from *Richard Rolle: The English Writings.*

Ruusbroec,[4] John, 1293–1381, of Brabant, priest, theologian, mystic, of the Rhineland School of spirituality. Quotations are taken from *John Ruusbroec: The Spiritual Espousals and Other Works.*

Safed Spirituality. Safed, a small town in the Galilean hills, which in the mid-16th century had a large Jewish population of the descendants of exiles from Spain and Portugal (who had been welcomed by Sultan Bayazid II), Jews from Syria, North Africa, Italy, and the Germanic states. Writings

---

4. LIBRARY OF CONGRESS NAME AUTHORITY: Ruusbroec, Jan van.

of the Safed Kabbalists are found in *Safed Spirituality: Rules of Mystical Piety, The Beginning of Wisdom.*

Sales, Francis de, 1547–1622, an aristocrat of Savoy, bishop, spiritual director, and reformer whose goal was a society infused with a spirit of true devotion. With Jane de Chantal he founded the Salesian School of spirituality. Selections are taken from his *Letters of Spiritual Direction.*

Savonarola, 1452–1498, Dominican preacher, visionary, and reformer, executed as a heretic and schismatic. Selections are taken from *Apocalyptic Spirituality*, a collection of writings of Lactantius, Adso, Joachim of Fiore, The Franciscan Spirituals, and Savonarola.

Shaker Manifesto, The. In *The Shakers: Two Centuries of Spiritual Reflection.*

Suso, Henry,[5] c. 1295–1366, Dominican, mystic, author of mystical texts in his vernacular (Middle High German), of the Rhineland School of spirituality, member of a group called Friends of God. Selections are taken from *Henry Suso: The Exemplar, with Two German Sermons.*

Symeon the New Theologian, 949–1022, Byzantine Christian, monk, reformer, mystic and theologian, exiled in 1009 for his charismatic teaching. Quotations are from *Symeon the New Theologian: The Discourses.*

Tauler, Johannes, c. 1300–1361, Dominican, mendicant preacher and spiritual director, mystic of the Rhineland

---

5. LIBRARY OF CONGRESS NAME AUTHORITY: Seuse, Heinrich.

School of spirituality, member of group called Friends of God. Selections are from *Johannes Tauler: Sermons.*

Teresa of Avila, 1515–1582, Carmelite, mystic, reformer, founder of convents of "discalced" Carmelites in Spain, teacher. Selections are from *Teresa of Avila: The Interior Castle.*

Thomas Aquinas, 1226–1274, Dominican theologian and contemplative. Often considered the finest systematic theologian of the western church. Quotations are taken from *Albert & Thomas: Selected Writings.*

Wesley, John, 1703–1791, spiritual leader in Bristol and London, translator of German Pietist hymns, preacher, founder of Methodism. Quotations are from *John and Charles Wesley: Selected Writings and Hymns.*

Wesley, Charles, 1707–1788, extraordinary hymn writer, spiritual leader, travelling preacher, social reformer. Quotations are from *John and Charles Wesley: Selected Writings and Hymns.*

"Winnebago Father's Teachings to His Son, A." In *Native North American Spirituality of the Eastern Woodlands.*

Woolman, John, 1720–1772. In *Quaker Spirituality: Selected Writings.*

Zohar, The. Written pseudononomously by a Spanish-Jewish Kabbalist, Moses de León, as an antique document. The Zohar is the major document of Kabbalah, the Jewish mystical tradition. Quotations are from *Zohar: The Book of Enlightenment,* which represents about two percent of the total work.

Appendix C
Using This Book/
Study Guide

In this Appendix we spell out for the reader or group leader some ways we have found helpful for using this text. The individual or group leader should feel free to modify as seems appropriate. This Appendix is comprised of two parts. The first part recommends the use of two preliminary exercises to sharpen a sense of the individual's spiritual journey. The second part looks to the actual use of the text individually or in a group.

a. Recalling your journey

Each participant is invited to engage in two preliminary exercises which are designed to sharpen perspectives on his or her own spiritual journey. If these exercises seem helpful, participants should spend several hours, preferably over a couple of days, retracing their personal journeys. Why do so? Do we know who we are and where we have come from? In many respects we do; yet in other regards our past is opaque and shifting. It is opaque in the sense that habits of nonreflectiveness, of over-attention to the present moment to the exclusion of attention to the flow of our lives, dulls our ability to see the sharp outlines of our own lives. As we begin again to pay attention to our own journeys we find forgotten and perhaps unconnected parts that spring to new life, and whose importance for the flow of our lives is only now discovered. Even for the habitually reflective person, the past is a shifting reality. Not that we can rewrite what has happened. Rather, as we move to new vantage points we begin to glimpse new vistas and have fresh insights. Marker events —birth of a grandchild, retirement, illness, financial need, death of a spouse, leaving the family home—all these open up new worlds that let us review other parts of our journey. For example, not only does retirement look very different when one has actually retired, but it is quite likely that one's whole life of working for a paycheck will take on new meaning and show us truths about ourselves that we have not known before.

We now turn to two questions which are designed to help us grasp the flow of our lives—inner and outer, inscape and landscape—with clarity.

1. Using your *left* hand (or your nondominant hand, if you prefer), draw a map of your spiritual journey. When you have done this for the first time please note for each stage the name you most commonly used for God, your preferred ways of praying, your devotions, your concerns, and those who were at that time like you. Note where you lived at the time, what you were doing, and what were the issues of the larger social world.
2. Describe changes in your spirituality during the past year or two. What has influenced these changes? What developments do you anticipate in the near future?

The first exercise has several parts. We begin by asking

you to draw a map of your spiritual journey, using your left or, if you prefer, your nondominant hand. Drawing with the left hand is a nonlinear, right-brain activity, intended to release some of the power of the imaginative, poetic self and free the self from the constriction of everyday logic. Some may wish to take a few deep breaths, literally and figuratively, to let the flow begin. The point is to engage your imagination and your memory, to begin to gather scattered fragments, to collect the stories and markers of a long journey. The configuration of the map may spark memories and help bring to light long-forgotten material.

Memories of a life lived do not come in an orderly progression; it takes time and structure to organize them into a coherent narrative. Hence our admonition to do this task for the first time over a few days. The map will shift as new inner voices clamor to be heard. The rest of this first exercise helps put in words some of the important elements of the spiritual life, and these items should be considered. Do not attack these exercises, though; let your mind wander gently and playfully over the inscape of a life lived. Jot down as much as you can. Never correct; there are no wrong answers. Write only for yourself at this point, without censoring.

The second exercise brings into focus your life as it now stands between an immediate past and an anticipated future. Be imaginative about the future. Let the future be more than a series of yesterdays and todays. Do not be afraid to create several scenarios—even frightening ones—which express your hopes and fears for the future.

At some point these or similar exercises are important, even urgent. Marc Kaminsky, writing about life review, says: "We can discern the life review process in action when we find, amid fragments of reminiscence, a recurring configuration of images that manifests a question and a partial answer to it."[1] Put in other words, "In the vast space of the imagination, it is possible to hold the past in the present, and youth in old age. The appeal to memory is a quest for meaning. In [our] solitude we create an account of [our] experience."[2] Our inner life and outer deeds of the past are not easily or immediately accessible; they are not like an outfit from 1925 that we can bring down from the attic. Our past needs constantly to be rewoven so that patterns emerge that show the questions we lived and our sometimes faltering, sometimes bold —but always partial—answer. We cannot give complete or even satisfactory responses in the present tense unless we are appropriately in touch with our past. That past from which our present emerges is often obscure. As you write and rewrite the story of your journey and your future you will be helped by memories which come unbidden, by dreams, by snippets of long-forgotten conversations, by old longings never satisfied, by touching again the hungers of flesh and of spirit which moved you.[3]

A few days later, when this task has been completed for the first time, the reader may move to the next section.

b. Using this book

In order to get started working with this book, it may be well for each participant personally to select one of the ques-

---

1. *The Uses of Reminiscence: New Ways of Working with Older Adults.* Edited by Marc Kaminsky. *Journal of Gerontological Social Work,* vol 7, 1/2. New York: Haworth Press, n.d., p. 13.

2. Text from the film *Water from Another Time.* Kane-Lewis Productions, 1982.

3. Those who wish to pursue the connection between their present spiritual life and their own past in a more structured way may find help in *The Practice of Process Meditation: The Intensive Journal Way to Spiritual Experience* by Ira Progoff. (New York: Dialogue House Library, 1980.)

tions addressed in it. We make no assumption that our order is best for someone else. The participant should spend about 15–30 minutes reflecting on his or her own life's answer to the selected question, making clear notes (either point or paragraph form). Although some people may experience a certain reluctance to write for themselves, these notes are invaluable. As progress occurs they serve to chart directions, to offer encouragement and insight. These exercises are a process of discovery. The surest way of saving and treasuring our discoveries involves both savoring them in our minds and hearts and committing them to paper.

This exercise may be initiated at a point where the participants are ready to work on their own, perhaps in the privacy of their own personal space, or a group of people may wish to find quiet spaces in which to work personally, before they return to speak with each other. This first step serves to help people become familiar with the process and initiates the process of conversation with themselves.

Whether a person is working individually or in a group, the next step is the same. It is now time to look on one's own at some of the selected quotes. Each quote is chosen because it answers the same question as that which is now engaging the person. These answers are taken from the writings in the Classics of Western Spirituality; they are words which try to express the insight of others of God's friends. If individuals are already confident of the approach to the spiritual life which is theirs, we invite them to read slowly and thoughtfully through the appropriate group of quotations and select one which on first reading seems attractive, challenging, or interesting. It is here that the dynamism of interaction with another begins. What does the selected quotation say to me? What insight does it add; how does it coincide with my line of approach; what *words*—individual words—are not part of my usual vocabulary; what is the "feel" of the text; do I think

I would like the person who wrote it; is it sympathetic with my gender perspective, and so on. Chew the text! Digest it! Engage it! It is important to take time at this point. While the approach of the chosen text may feel comfortable, it is often difficult to appropriate its content. I may, for example, be comfortable with the approach of Julian of Norwich's statement: "For our courteous Lord does not want his servants to despair because they fall often and grievously; for our falling does not hinder him in loving us" (p. 245). It is quite a different matter, however, to let the sense of her message penetrate and challenge my own feelings of guilt and self-reproach.

When this first task is complete, it is time to ask the second question: What does my answer say to enrich the other's perspective? Obviously the text you are reading is not a complete articulation of *all possible answers.* You have something to add, even to the words of Teresa of Avila or Augustine! Engage yourself in this part of the dialogue with respect for the wisdom of the other and respect for your own insight. God's gracious spirit is working through you, too.

It is important that the answers be written—they form a record of starting points. Even the best and most refreshing or revealing insight can slip away if it is not written down. Imagine if a person lost in a fire a life's worth of diaries! The parallel is appropriate—it is possible in this process to grasp a life insight which will stay with us only for a moment, like a dream captured upon waking. Do not lose the insight. Do not waste it. Do not judge right now whether it will be of worth later on.

Working in a group

The group must decide what question it wishes to work on as a group. This may be a question which some have already answered or it may be a new question. Each person takes time to answer the question personally and to write an initial answer. When the process is first engaged, this may only take 15 minutes or so; later, it will take more time as people become more used to engaging and being engaged by the quotes and by the interaction with their own answers. A person who finishes quickly may wish to take a second quote to work with. When the group is ready, each participant should begin by indicating from which group they chose a quotation. If the group is large enough that there are at least three persons in each type of approach to the spiritual life, it may be well for each subgroup to meet together to share whatever they wish of their personal answers, the quotation they selected, and their response to this quotation. If the group is small, each participant should be invited to share what they wish to of their answer, to read the quotation they selected, and to share their reflections on it.

The process may be less threatening in subgroups which share a common approach to the spiritual life. If there are not enough people taking part in the exercise, the leader may wish to remind all concerned that they are not to quarrel with or question someone else's answer. Critique of a personal answer is a personal task. It is this which is engaged in the next step.

Whether individually or in a group, each person is invited to look to the group of quotations which is polar opposite to the one from which they took their preferred quotation. From this group they are invited to select a quotation for reflection and written response. Thus a person who favors the heart/imaging approach should go to the mind/emptying of images group and vice versa, and the person who favors the heart/emptying of images approach should go to the mind/imaging group of quotations and vice versa. This step sometimes brings a certain discomfort with it. Generally we do not engage easily in the type of approach to the spiritual life which is opposite to ours. We do not much like to have our set-in ways disturbed; we are more comfortable burrowing in more deeply to our preferred style. This is, however, a critical step. Individuals and group participants will usually go along, albeit somewhat begrudgingly, because they recognize that a complementary approach will both enrich theirs and challenge its limitations.

When this phase is complete, and if there is time and energy to continue at this point, the individual or the group may either select another quotation to work with or go on to a new question. If there is not much time and energy, a little time should be spent bringing closure. After a time of quiet, each person should write a sentence or phrase, or even a word of thanksgiving. When time is available—either at this moment or at a later hour or day—each may wish to return to work with the preliminary exercises noted at the beginning of this Appendix; the answers to these will evolve as each question is answered, each quotation engaged, each opposite perspective allowed to bring us to a sense of the limits of our very real gifts in the presence of the Divine Mystery.

Appendix D
Spiritual Approaches and Personality Types

*T*he modern division of personalities into eight different psychological types was proposed by Carl Jung in the 1920s, and developed by Katherine Briggs and Isabel Briggs Myers in the now familiar Myers-Briggs Type Indicator (1962) in which sixteen distinct types of personalities are distinguished. Just before her death, Isabel Briggs Myers published her further findings and conclusions in *Gifts Differing*. The title of that book puts in sharp relief the heart of the conclusions reached by these researchers and others: human personalities differ, and each personality type is well described as a "gift differing."

In this brief explanation, we isolate only two sets of variables (called functions), namely, sensation and intuition, and thinking and feeling. The decision to isolate two sets of functions is based not only on limitations of space; it also allows us to put into relief the polarities described by Holmes which we followed.

The first set of functions, sensation and intuition, are those functions through which we perceive, or register, the input of data from the outside world. Sensation basically relies on the perception of the five senses and most easily perceives concrete objects and facts (how things are). Sensation shows a preference for sensory reality, details, immediacy and concreteness. Intuition, on the other hand, is characterized as perception by way of the unconscious. Intuition looks toward the inner meaning of events and their possible implications and effects; it brings the dimension of the future into focus, and is concerned with the possibilities and consequences of what is happening rather than present facts in themselves. Intuition shows a preference for possibilities, patterns, change, anticipation, and vision. "The sensation-preferring or 'sensible' person wants facts, trusts facts, and remembers facts. [. . .] The intuitive finds appeal in the metaphor and enjoys vivid imagery. The possible is always in front of him [or her] pulling on his [or her] imagination like a magnet."[1]

The second set of functions is feeling and thinking. These are called the rational functions because they assess what is brought to the individual through sensation or intuition. They organize perceptions and suggest to the individual how to act in response. Feelers make decisions based on their own deepest feelings and their reading of the feelings of others. Feelers grasp the world through an evaluation based on felt values and personal impact. Feelers prefer subjective values, and find the significant aspects of reality to be feeling, memory, ideals. Thinkers use the information they have taken in to make decisions based on reason, logic, or systematic thought-processes. The thinker is comfortable with an impersonal basis for decisions, and prefers to rely on impartial, objective judgment. Thinkers prefer objective values, and find theory and principles to be significant aspects of reality.

---

1. David Keirsey & Marilyn Bates, *Please Understand Me*, Del Mar, CA: Prometheus Nemesis Books, 1978, pp. 17–18.

The first polarity (non-imaging/imaging) is related to the intuition/sensation continuum. While all people are to some degree both sensate and intuitive, most people also have a preferred function: they perceive reality and grasp facts *in the first instance* either in the arena of the spirit/ imagination or of the body/facts; that is, with an intuition about how things are or by a piecing together of the picture from sense data (touching, seeing, hearing, etc.). The second polarity (heart/mind) is related to the feeling/thinking continuum. While all people both think and feel, most people also have a preferred function: they make judgments about reality *in the first instance* in the primary arena of either heart or mind: feeling judges people and things as good or bad, attractive or unattractive; thinking judges statements as true or false. These preferred ways of appropriating reality and coping with problems and tasks results from our psychological givens, and are shaped by early experience, education, church tradition, and so on.

Four approaches:

Imaging/feeling (SF[2]). Some will tend to approach the spiritual life in a feeling manner and with rich imagery: their orientation is affective. The means or techniques they use involve images in meditation, feeling worship, small-group relations. In this group, feeling is dominant; they stress meditative prayer leading to presence, and try to model God's reign and be signs of it. In its excessive form this position will

---

2. SF, NF, ST, NT refer to the Myers-Briggs typology: sensate-feeling, intuitive-feeling, sensate-thinking, intuitive-thinking.

tend toward emotionalism and excessive concern for feelings and right experience.

Emptying/feeling (NF). Other persons will tend to approach the spiritual life equally in a feeling manner, but by emptying of sense images: their orientation is also affective; their goal is also illumination of the heart, but the means or techniques used will involve non-imaginal contemplation leading to mystical union, intuition, quiet worship with more inner prayer. This group may seek to live a contemplative life away from the world. In its excessive form this position will tend to a neglect of the culture and an excessive concern for absorption into God.

Imaging/thinking (ST). A third group of people will tend to approach the spiritual life in a thinking manner and with rich imagery: their orientation is intellectual or speculative, seeking illumination of the mind; they will use techniques engaging the senses in meditation which images. However, in this group intellect is dominant, and they will stress mental prayer leading to insight, involvement with the world, study groups and better sermons. In excess this position will tend to dogmatism and an excessive concern for reason and right thinking.

Emptying/thinking (NT). The fourth group will approach the spiritual life equally in a thinking manner, but by emptying of sense images: their orientation is also intellectual or speculative, seeking illumination of the mind. However, they will use techniques of non-imaginal contemplation, emptying the senses. This group will stress active prayer leading to witness, they will strive to build God's reign and witness to it, they will desire more social, active and relevant worship. Will is dominant for this group, and in its excessive form this position tends to prophetic judgment on culture and excessive concern for right action.

Prayer, personality type, and diversity

It may come as a surprise to some that others approach the spiritual life so differently from them. Personality type is a powerful if little remarked factor in the spiritual life. The spiritual life is a human experience, the experience of God is known in the human mind and heart, and a principal foundation of the spiritual life is personality type. There are, of course, other foundations: the whole complexus of individual psychologies, educational background, religious tradition, and cultural heritage. Personality type identifies dimensions of the way we relate to ourselves, others, and the world. Clarity about one's starting points in these matters reassures us about the validity of individual differences. Attention to individual differences breeds respect for other options, other starting points, while at the same time probably indicating one principal reason why we find certain texts and certain authors unmoving, why we have trouble getting engaged with these authors, and perhaps why many of our attempts at prayer (for example) have been so fruitless. Attention to one's starting point also points to an appropriate corrective to excesses and a path to growth.

The psychology of personality type speaks of inferior functions (the polar opposite of one's preference) as a necessary balance. Each type of approach to the spiritual life ought to be balanced by its polar opposite. Thus the imaging/feeling type should be balanced by the emptying/thinking type (and vice versa) and the emptying/feeling type ought to be balanced by the imaging/thinking type. At times this will not be an easy discipline.

These two insights, namely type of approach and the need to be balanced by the polar opposite type have had some influence on the shape of this book. We do not rely on a Myers-Briggs typology, however. As useful as this may be for some, it has been deemed more satisfactory to work with a simpler typology of two scales, four approaches as seen in the explanation in chapter one. A particular caution about the use of Myers-Briggs typology is found in *From Image to Likeness*. The maturing individual gradually incorporates all dimensions of personality. Any once-for-all-time typing is likely to be static rather than dynamic. Human persons are, of course, dynamic if they are living and growing.

Nevertheless, there is much to be learned from the study of personality type and spiritual approach. For those who wish to pursue further this relationship, the following bibliography may be of interest.

Bryant, Christopher, *Prayer and Different Types of People*. Gainesville, FL: Center for Applications of Psychological Type, Inc., 1983.

Campbell, Joseph, ed., *The Portable Jung*. New York: Viking Press, 1971, pp. 178–269.

von Franz, Marie-Louise and James Hillman, *Jung's Typology*. Dallas, TX: Spring Publications, 1971.

Grant, W. Harold, Magdala Thompson and Thomas E. Clarke, *From Image to Likeness, a Jungian Path in the Gospel Journey*. New York: Paulist, 1983.

Keating, Charles J., *Who We Are Is How We Pray*. Mystic, CT: Twenty-Third Publications, 1987.

Keirsey, David and Marilyn Bates, *Please Understand Me*. Del Mar, CA: Prometheus Nemesis Books, 1978.

Lawrence, Gordon, *People Types and Tiger Stripes.* Gainesville, FL: Center for Applications of Psychological Type, Inc., n.d.

Michael, Chester P. and Marie C. Norrisey, *Prayer and Temperament.* Charlottesville, VA: The Open Door, Inc., 1984.

Myers, Isabel Briggs, *Gifts Differing.* Palo Alto, CA: Consulting Psychologists Press, Inc., 1980.

————, *Introduction to Type.* Palo Alto, CA: Consulting Psychologists Press, Inc., 1985.

Page, Earle C., "Finding Your Spiritual Path, Following Your Spiritual Path." Gainesville, FL: Center for Applications of Psychological Type, Inc., 1982.

Repicky, Robert A., "Jungian Typology and Christian Spirituality." *Review for Religious,* 40, 1981, pp. 422–435.

Schemel, George J. and James A. Borbely, *Facing Your Type.* Wernersville, PA: Typofile, 1982.